Like an ancient relic resurrected for the modern day, Carleena intelligently weaves together wisdom from across many traditions so that we can lovingly find our way back home to ourselves-no matter what season of life we find our feet in. This will be a reference guide for humanity for years to come!

— SARAH GRADY, DOULA & AUTHOR OF
*HOMECOMING: A FEMININE GPS FOR A
LOST WORLD*

Carleena's work is deep + profound yet feels like an accessible homecoming to the truth of what makes life worth truly living. With each chapter, comes a real sense of knowing who and what we get to be when we unlock our innate expression through wisdom rooted in rhythm with nature's cycles.

— LUNA MAYE, SOUND THERAPY
PRACTITIONER, RECORDING +
PERFORMANCE ARTIST

Cyclical living is indeed the key to unlocking not just our ancient wisdom, but the natural process by which we can easefully and enjoyably create all that we deeply desire. This beautiful bit of alchemy by Carleena Lara Bregatta transforms universal wisdom into the simple, user-friendly guide we humans need to tap into the magic that is already within and around us.

> — ADRIENNE MACIAIN, PH.D., AUTHOR
> OF *SPARK GENIUS: CREATIVE FLOW*
> *UNLEASHED*

A remedy for what ails us; this masterful book is a powerful invitation back to ourselves and back to how we each *could* be. By charting a cyclical rhythm and offering so many entry points into a new relationship with ourselves this book guarantees lasting transformation for its readers.

> — SIERRA MELCHER, AUTHOR OF *HOW*
> *CHANGE REALLY HAPPENS & DATE*
> *YOURSELF*

As I opened the first page of The Akashic Alchemist I arrived into an awakening in my body and womb, a profound wave of knowing spiralled within me, I had opened a portal of divine feminine wisdom. Carleena has brought the intricate wisdom of the feminine to us in the pages of her book in a way that is digestible and allows space for the awakening of each individual woman to unfold through her words and wisdom. Having the honour to bear witness to Carleena in her full creative process and birthing of her book I can share that she is not only the carrier of deep wisdom but she is also the living, breathing embodiment of all she shares.

— REBECCA WILSON, WOMEN'S GUIDE,
MENTOR AND SPIRITUAL MIDWIFE
THROUGH THE SEASONS OF LIFE,
RITES OF PASSAGE AND WOMANHOOD

THE AKASHIC ALCHEMIST

A CYCLICAL GUIDE TO REMEMBERING YOUR SOUL'S ANCIENT WISDOM

CARLEENA LARA BREGATTA

Em,
I love you sistr
♡ Carleena

Red Thread Publishing LLC. 2023

Write to info@redthreadbooks.com if you are interested in publishing
with Red Thread Publishing. Learn more about publications or foreign
rights acquisitions of our catalog of books: www.redthreadbooks.com

Paperback ISBN: 978-1-955683-47-0

Ebook ISBN: 978-1-955683-48-7

Original Cover Art: Prism + Fleur, Paige McLeod

@prism.and.fleur www.prismandfleur.com

Author Photo © Julia Lehman @julialehmanart

*The information and advice contained in this book are based upon the research and
the personal and professional experiences of the author. They are not intended as a
substitute for consulting with a healthcare professional. The publisher and author are
not responsible for any adverse effects or consequences resulting from the use of any of
the suggestions, preparations, or procedures discussed in this book. All matters
pertaining to your physical health should be supervised by a healthcare professional.*

CONTENTS

To the people who gave me life.

THE AKASHIC ALCHEMIST

Akasha [noun] (**sanskrit**): *a universal etheric field or dimension in which a record of all past, present and future events is imprinted, recorded and remembered; ether/space*

Alchemist [noun]: *a person who transforms or creates something through a seemingly magickal process; someone who enjoys the fruits of inner transformation through healing and freeing inner parts of selves, leading to liberation from fear and outdated beliefs*

Magick [noun]: *the process of aligning oneself with natural forces and Inner Alchemy to manifest an intention. [note: This is different than the spelling of 'magic' which is typically used to describe fictional energy in fantasy and films.]*

ALCHEMICAL SYMBOLS

WATER

AIR

FIRE

EARTH

METAL (GOLD)

INTEGRATION (TAIJITU)

INTRODUCTION

EN ESPANOL [SPANISH TRANSLATION]	EN INGLÉS [ENGLISH TRANSLATION]
Caminaré en belleza	*I will walk in beauty*
Caminaré en paz	*I will walk in peace*
Caminaré en belleza	*I will walk in beauty*
Caminaré en paz	*I will walk in peace*
Todo es mi familia	*Everything is my family*
Todo es mi familia	*Everything is my family*
Todo es sagrado	
Las plantas y animales	*Everything is sacred*
Todo es sagrado	*Animals and plants*
Las montañas y el mar	*Everything is sacred*
	Mountains and the sea
Todo es mi familia	*Everything is my family*
Todo es mi familia	*Everything is my family*
Heya heya heya	*Heya heya heya*
Heya heya hey	*Heya heya hey*
Heya heya heya	*Heya heya heya*
Heya heya hey	*Heya heya hey*
Todo es mi familia	*Everything is my family*
Todo es mi familia	*Everything is my family*
Todos somos familia	*We are all family*

Todo es mi familia by Alonso del Río

INTRODUCTION

Indigenous Earth-based cultures throughout cosmic time have understood that we are not simply in nature, but *are* nature. The water that spirals through your body most likely came from asteroids. The fresh vegetables and fruits you eat soaked up their life force from the sun. We're blessed that the very air we breathe didn't slough off the very edge of the Earth and instead coalesced into a liveable greenhouse that we know as our atmosphere, absorbed through the branch like tendrils of your lungs. Sometimes it is easy to forget that the very existence of life – metaphorically represented as this breath you're taking right now – is indeed a miracle. This awareness, of sensing this precious life as a miracle, was not something I always believed. Rather, I came here knowing, forgot, and then remembered again.

When I think of the last time I remembered, I was a child. She had her hands in the dirt often, exploring every inch of the ivy-infused land surrounding my family's rancher, listening to the songs of the plants. She'd nurse earthworms back to life in her bug hospital; the unsuspecting victims that accidentally got split open by her toy shovel would of course be tended to. The fireflies that speckled the royal blue sky just after sunset reminded her of the myriad of stars in the Milky Way. She'd lie on her back and wonder which ones she's visited in previous lives. Slipping into the dream realm, she learned how to pray and ask for what she wanted, manifesting as lucid dreams where she was the conductor of her visions. In her waking state she could sense and feel how others were feeling and thinking. She didn't see her ability to sense the pulse of the world as a burden, but a gift. She knew this all without needing to open her third eye.

Growing up my nickname was Beana (*Vina in Spanish*) and Beana loved making mud pies with her sister Ria. Long before the advent of YouTube, we'd pretend to have our own little cooking show in our sunflower wallpaper kitchen, teaching the imaginary audience how to make the most perfect PB&J. My inner child was an unabashed witch of the woods who wanted to explore every corner of the world, learn from her land and teach others how to make the most delicious sandwich to an audience of many. She believed that anything was possible.

She's not exactly sure when this happened, but there came a time when her childhood ebbed, contracting its tendrils of "reality" around her. Complex life experiences, which western medicine may classify as trauma, accumulated in the muscles, fascia and bones of her body. Significant and subtle experiences began filtering her life and an armor developed around her heart. Beana slowly began to believe it just wasn't safe to be the light that she was in a world that seemed to have so much darkness.

As these life experiences tumbled into her life like the cartwheels she used to do instead of walking places, a density began to clog the communication between her mind and her heart. The world had become a seemingly scary place that she had to protect herself from. Sometimes she'd sit up and wonder, *when did life get so hard? Can't we just go back to making potions in the woods?* Beana was unofficially initiated, passing through the portal of childhood and into "the real world," reborn as Carleena.

The lucid dreams where she could become a mermaid or fly at will ceased and were replaced with restless sleep. Her ability to sense and perceive others' emotions and thoughts felt overwhelming, and so she chose – on some level – for her psychic senses to withdraw. She learned a lot from the world around her and developed a perception of her place within it. At some point she radically declared, "*yes, this world* is *fucked and so am I.*"

Living through global events like 9/11, COVID-19 and quarantine, global warming threatening humanity's future and realizing that 2 companies own mostly all of the toxic products that the average American household consumes, it's easy for me to think sometimes…*Yes, this world is indeed fucked!*

Deep within my heart though there is another voice that keeps its innocent curiosity.
What if things could work out the way I desire them to?
What if we have the power to choose a new way?
What if I was still that little alchemist, able to conjure the world I'd want my children to live in?

My journey of becoming an Akashic Alchemist began in 2012 – the year of my awakening. But it wasn't an awakening like I'd read through the perspectives of Eckhart Tolle or the Buddha where suddenly all was clear. My awakening was the transitional point in life where I hit rock bottom and knew I could no longer live my life on autopilot, believing everything was fucked. It wasn't until the shadows literally surrounded me, almost strangling me to death to wake me up, the story of which I tell in *Part 1: Your Inner Winter.* It was the moment in time when I began to reclaim responsibility over my life.

Through learning how to navigate my personal dark night of the soul, I came to see how I was living my life on autopilot, letting my life just happen as if I was watching it from the sidelines. That year, in the dark winter of 2012, I began placing myself back in the driver's seat of my life and recognized how I needed to address the pain that was caused from abandoning myself, and my inner child, along my life path.

Before my awakening I was on track to becoming a psychotherapist who was inspired by the thought of prestigious academic recognition; publication in peer-reviewed articles was my five to ten year plan. I had renounced my Catholic faith long before this and had developed into quite a staunch atheist, believing in the pseudo-religion of Science instead, having no spiritual practice within me. I thought that perhaps I'd be a neuroscientist, or maybe a speaker for the United Nations. The version of me then could not have even dreamt of this version of me now.

The version of me now is an 800 Hour E-RYT (Experienced Registered Yoga Teacher), Reiki Master, Hypnotherapist and Somatic Coach. I help people repattern limiting subconscious beliefs, recover from trauma and find safety, sovereignty and freedom in their lives. I have been teaching and writing about spirituality, meditation, philosophy and self empowerment for a decade. That 2012 version of me would not believe that I could have created a soul-led business and be working for myself, but each precious moment of my life built upon the last, guiding me home to my purpose.

I share this with you because no matter where you are in life, in your healing journey, you are on the right path. Your soul will always guide you home. And it is my hope that this book and the teachings of *The Akashic Alchemist* will nurture you along your journey home.

I will not lie to you though: this book will not answer your life's questions, nor can it solve any of your current struggles. What the book may do is inspire you to dig deep and remember the ancient wisdom that you have held within you all along.

Throughout this book, at the end of each chapter, you will see a section called Alchemical Tools. Alchemical Tools are tangible things you can add into your healing practices so that you can remember the wisdom that is within you. Alchemy means creating internal transformation through healing and freeing inner parts of selves, leading to liberation from fear and outdated beliefs.

What will you be transforming? First, you may transform your relationship from linear living to cyclical living, beginning to see your evolution as a spiral outward, rather than a straight and upward line. You will learn the reasons why cyclical living can increase your energy and capacity for life, create more connection to yourself and the world around you and inspire compassion and self love. You will do this through learning about the archetypal Inner Seasons of Winter, Spring, Summer, Late Summer and Autumn. *(Throughout this book you will notice certain words being capitalized. Every time you see a capitalized letter on a word, it is there to clarify that I am talking about archetypal energy that can be used for Inner Alchemy. When the name of a Season is capitalized, I am talking about the symbolic Season, rather than the literal season.)* Archetypal Seasons are your Inner Seasons that may or may not occur during the literal season. For example, you may be navigating an Inner Winter – the symbolic time when we transmute our past memories (like trauma) and learn how to inner resource safety – despite it being summer outside. When you can identify what Inner Season you're in, you can enjoy alchemy practices that support your growth, evolution and healing journey.

Secondly, you may transform your relationship to your Emotions which each correspond to a particular Season, namely Winter = Fear; Spring = Anger; Summer = Joy; Late Summer = Empathy; Autumn = Grief. This book will not teach you ways to get rid of your Emotions, but ways to rebuild and repair your relationship with them, to perhaps come to see them as ancient and loving teachers, holding wisdom and guidance for you.

Lastly, what may transform is your connection to this planet, our Great Mother Earth through reading more about the magick of the Elements. Magick is the process of aligning oneself with natural forces and Inner Alchemy to manifest an intention. These natural forces I describe as the Elements of Water, Wood, Fire, Earth and Metal.

This book is heavily inspired by Five Element Theory. Five Element Theory, also known as the Five Phases or Five Elements, is a foundational concept in Traditional East Asian Medicine and philosophy. It categorizes the natural phenomena and patterns of the world into these five Elements, representing interconnected aspects of nature, organs in the human body, Emotions, Seasons, and other aspects of life, illustrating their dynamic and cyclical relationships.

Archetypal Elements refer to universal symbols or themes that are deeply ingrained in human consciousness and appear across cultures and time. They represent fundamental patterns, or primordial forces, which serve as structures for understanding and interpreting human experiences and behavior. Other cultures and ancient traditions may call these archetypal energies by other names, and you are welcome to use your own frameworks interchangeably with them.

HOW TO READ THIS BOOK

As you read, use your discernment and give yourself permission to question things. You are the alchemist of your life and you get to choose how you want your spiritual and healing journey to look and feel like. The teachings in this book are one way, out of many ways, to empower feelings of freedom and liberation. May this living transmission of work be a messenger that relays to you: *you are whole, you have always been whole, and you will always be whole. Here is one way to remember.*

As I mentioned earlier, this book may not solve your current struggles, nor may it provide you with earth-shattering answers. What it may do is inspire aligned action and empower you to fall back in love with yourself and the planet. This book is only one part of the puzzle within the work of art that is your healing journey. Written word helps our cognitive mind understand and remember concepts, but that is not all of who you are! You are a multifaceted soul having a human experience, so we must not only speak to the mind, but to the body, heart *and* soul.

To that end I've created special tools for you to practice as you go along. Speckled throughout this book are invitations to head to the book's website at www. carleenalarayoga.com/the-akashic-alchemist (Password: Alchemist999) to enjoy guided meditations, embodiment/movement practices, hypnotherapy sessions and worksheets with journal prompts and exercises.

Neuroscientists postulate that when we are wanting to create long-lasting shifts in our perceptions, beliefs, habits and perspectives, we want to include the physical body in the practice[1]. As we go through this book, which is organized metaphorically and symbolically by the Seasons, you will learn tangible practices, called Alchemical Tools, that involve your physical body (aka soma), mind, heart *and* soul. I recommend trying on some of these practices to enhance the transformational power of this book.

When you're going through this journey for the first time, I do recommend skimming or reading in the order that the teachings are presented, as the tools I introduce build upon the last. For example, we start in Inner Winter because this Season teaches us how to regulate our nervous system. A regulated nervous system is a necessary foundation to build upon that supports all of the practices that come later in further Seasons. After your first read or skim through, when you want to come back to the book and take a deeper dive, feel free to jump around based on your Inner Season, or be guided by your intuition.

The Akashic Alchemist pilgrimage begins in **Cycle One: Inner Winter**, which is the Season of life when you learn from the Emotion of Fear. Significant life events, such as surviving trauma, can affect a healthy Fear response, so you'll learn the importance of nervous system regulation and resourcing inner safety to create a supportive foundation for you. Inner Winter is ruled by the Water Element, which is where your subconscious memories are stored. You'll learn how to receive the gifts of Inner Winter which are trust, memory and intuition.

In **Cycle Two: Inner Spring**, you will learn from the Emotion of Anger. Anger arises when something in life is not what you want it to be and can often arise when we encounter life's obstacles. You'll learn how to transmute frustration into aligned action to bring you this Season's gifts of motivation, direction and focused attention. This phase is ruled by an Element called Wood which can be interchangeable with Wind.

Cycle Three: Inner Summer is an expansive journey where you will learn from the Emotion of Joy. Joy, within the context of *The Akashic Alchemist*, is more about contentment than ecstasy. You'll unpack your relationship to Joy during this Season, enjoying alchemical practices that will bring you this Season's gifts of belonging, authenticity and play. Like the radiant days of summer, this Season is ruled by the Fire Element.

Our journey then continues to **Cycle Four: The Space Between**, which is a nuanced phase. The Space Between has two meanings: it is also known as "Late Summer," and is also the bridge between every Inner Season. There is a subtle and stable energy nurturing you between all the Seasons, supporting healthy change and transition. The Space Between is ruled by the Earth Element and our Emotional Teacher is Empathy. The physical matter of our bodies and DNA represent the gifts of ancestral healing and abundance, which can be harnessed through Inner Alchemy.

The last Season we navigate is **Inner Autumn** which is ruled by an Element called Metal. Metal aligns perfectly to this Season, because when you tap into its magick, you receive its gifts of preciousness, worthiness and liberation. This cycle's Emotional Teacher is Grief as we alchemize our capacity to let life in and let go of attachments, without bypassing.

I have also included a closing chapter called **Integration**, which provides you with tools on digesting this book for sustainable change, promoting an empowered transformation within yourself and your relationship to this planet. After a decade of teaching and holding space within the spiritual community, I have noticed a need for integration. After we learn large amounts of new information and concepts, we may need some time to digest the material and practice it. This final chapter will inspire you to take aligned action in your life to integrate the information in this book.

For readers who want to take their integration one step further, or wish to dive deeper into alchemical work, you are invited to join our online membership community where we gather monthly for private calls. These calls are welcoming and expansive places where you can connect with soul family – aka other readers of this book – who are interested in similar topics and subjects as you. Members also have private access to healing techniques (such as yoga practices, meditations, hypnotherapy journeys and somatic embodiment practices) that go beyond the ones that are offered in the book. More information on the membership portal is shared on the book's website. This website page is intended to be for readers of this book. Thank you for keeping this work confidential and private.

Website URL:
www.carleenalarayoga.com/the-akashic-alchemist
Website Password: Alchemist999
Linktree: linktr.ee/theakashicalchemist
(see QR code to scan)

CYCLE ONE: INNER WINTER

THE WOMB OF NO THING

Our journey begins with the spiral inwards
to the watery world of Inner Winter.

The dark womb where no-thing
and everything
exists.

A paradox
of simultaneously knowing the expansive wisdom of the
multiverse
and resting softly
without knowing a thing.

Your Inner Winter is a safe space
where you'll gather your courage for what is to come,
but not before you rest.

For now, it is time
to surrender yourself
back down
into the belly of the Earth.

Don't worry, my love.
All will be waiting for you when you awaken.
You have spent ten thousand lifetimes
expanding into all that you believe yourself to be.

How deserving you are of such rest.

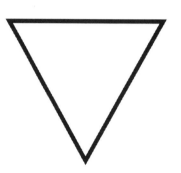

INNER WINTER AT A GLANCE

PRIMARY ELEMENT
Water

PRIMARY EMOTIONS
Fear

RELATED CHAKRA
Sacral (*Svadhishthana*)

GIFTS OF THE SEASON
Feeling safe
Trusting others/trusting the
universe
Peace that arises from stillness
Positive relationship with rest
Courageous (fearful but doing it
anyway)
Intuitive
Ability to surrender
Curious About the mystery of life

**DIVINE FEMININE SHADOW OF
FEAR**
Waiting for the other shoe to drop
Overly controlling, cautious or
protective
Difficulty trusting others/the world
Paralyzed by fear
Anxious

**DIVINE MASCULINE SHADOW
OF FEAR**
Resisting rest
Ruthless drive for external power
Fearless/reckless
God complex

**PHYSICAL MANIFESTATIONS OF
FEAR**
Kidney/urinary bladder issues
Adrenal issues
Dysregulated nervous system
Problems with legs/ankles/knees
Pelvic floor/reproductive issues
Chronic ear infections/ear issues
Bone/teeth/hair issues

TRAUMA
Physical, emotional or sexual abuse
Childhood trauma
Continued nervous system
dysregulation
Birth trauma
Medical procedures
Life threatening illness diagnoses
Bullying/harassment
Exposure to violence/abuse/death

INNER WINTER AT A GLANCE

ALCHEMY PRACTICES

Nervous system regulation
Shadow work
Breathwork
Somatic exercises
Emotional release techniques
Embodiment
Yoga
Yoga nidra
Hypnotherapy
Journaling

AFFIRMATIONS

At this moment, all my needs are met.
I am safe.
I trust myself.
Everything is always working out for me.
I am always protected.

I SURVIVED

"The Tao is dark and unfathomable.
How can it make her radiant?
Because she lets it...
This source is called darkness.
The gateway to all understanding."
- Tao Te Ching by Laozi

I t wasn't the craziest thing to have my ex-boyfriend
show up at my house in the middle of the night.
Although...part of me *was* confused as to how he
made it all the way up to my bedroom on the third floor of
my college apartment without me letting him in. Behind
my bedroom's locked door, he adjusted his voice to sound
like he was crying and that he urgently needed to speak to
me. Trusting, I opened the door.

I was met with a version of a man that my inner child
would equate to a monster. His demeanor was entirely
different from the saddened boy whom I thought wanted
my comfort, whom I had previously imagined was standing
behind the door just a moment ago. Instead, I saw his

lifeless eyes look into mine just for a moment, before he lunged at my neck to strangle me.

A wordless battle of willpower ensued in my magenta pink bedroom, perched on the third floor of my college apartment. We wrestled and I clawed as we worked our way around the room. Breaking my coffee table from him slamming me into it. Scattering my tchotchkes of owl statues and bowls holding jewelry around my sacred space. I used every ounce of strength I had to fight for my life.

He was significantly larger and stronger than me, yet my will to live was mightier. My sympathetic nervous system was online, allowing me the gift of awareness of watching his every move – despite the chaos, I was ready for anything. Catching a split second moment when his guard was down, his feet not firmly planted on the floor, I seized it. Tripping him over his own two feet, I pushed him backwards as he struggled to hold on to me and break his fall. He reached out as if I'd catch him. Instead of holding on to him like I always did, with a final kick, I shoved him out my bedroom door, locking it behind him.

Pounding on the door, he ruthlessly tried to get back into my room, but those doors from an 1800s West Chester Pennsylvania home are stronger than they make 'em these days. The barrier of wood and metal didn't budge, although all of me felt afraid it would. For hours he'd dance this dance of pretending to leave, slamming the front door, silently walk back up the three flights of stairs, jiggle my bedroom door handle, scream at me, and repeat the cycle again. This pattern of trying to finish what he started continued until the sun came up, when at last he went home.

For the two weeks that followed I had skipped all of my classes, hunkered in my room to avoid anyone seeing my black eyes and bruises. I felt nauseatingly anxious and continuously petrified. I wasn't ready for the world to see this strange version of me, deeply ashamed of what others may think. I flitted between states of extreme fear and numbing dissociation. Throughout that time many parts of me wondered: how the *hell* did I end up here?

As I wrestled with my own shadows, I prayed every day for relief from my suffering. They were the type of prayers that bring you to your knees and have you praying to a God that you're not even sure you believe in. Oftentimes I'd be curled up in fetal pose on the floor in my bedroom, face dampened by the incessant tears that fell, rocking myself to sleep. Other times I'd pace around my room, obsessively checking the locks and looking out the blinds, scanning for anything suspicious. After one week of tenderly navigating my dark night of the soul, I knew I had to pull myself out of this deep, dark well I was in. It was time to start picking up the pieces.

While on that unofficial sabbatical from University, I intuitively found ways to keep my mind focused on something other than my limiting beliefs and alleviate the mounting tension in my body. I created some of my favorite pieces of art and wrote plenty of poetry that would make any Sylvia Plath fan proud. As I recently had a friend download p90x workout videos on my laptop, I decided to keep my blood flowing through online exercise videos instead of pacing around my room. The fiery practices burned off so much of the boiling energy in my body and empowered me to believe I was getting stronger.

This cold week in February, just after Valentine's Day of 2012, was when I discovered yoga. I had a profound experience at the end of that first yoga class, which was a prerecorded video part of the workout series. My first *savasana* – which is the final resting pose at the end of a yoga asana practice – opened up a portal from my human self to my soul, activating hope and initiating me to keep going.

As I lay on my bedroom floor, I drifted into a dimension of inner bliss where my identity – and all of the limiting beliefs that came with it – entirely slipped away. All of my worries melted out of my mind and into the Earth, melting off of me like honey. My inner landscape became clear of conscious thought. I was held in the warmth of my own presence. For those moments suspended in time, I was liberated from my suffering.

Savasana, meaning corpse pose in Sanskrit, has a few different metaphorical meanings and intentions. At its core, corpse pose is symbolic of the energetic deaths that we encounter throughout our life. New versions of you are being born all the time, as old versions naturally phase themselves out. *Savasana* invites you to subtly become more familiar and acquainted with death while honoring the death of who you were before you practiced.

During my first yoga class, resting close to the Earth, I felt how appropriate this pose's name is. My yoga practice found me exactly when I needed it, arriving as an unconscious manifestation to help me mend my fractured heart during a time when I contemplated leaving my body for good. Corpse pose arrived to give me the shamanic death that I actually needed. A part of me did die that day and, ironically, that death liberated me. In a way I remembered how much I wanted to live. I didn't know it at the time, but my prayers to be liberated from my darkness were being answered. I was having my first spiritual awakening of this lifetime, ushered into the most transformative of Inner Winters.

Inner Winter is about rewriting the narratives that have run their course, releasing threads that have bound you to blaming yourself, or blaming the world. You can consider

Inner Winter as the fertile void from which new, supportive and loving kind beliefs will sprout. It is the space where everything materializes, and is simultaneously, the same place where all later dies. This obsidian cave is where you can locate your inner sense of safety, just like that *savasana*, soaking in feelings of love, compassion and ease that are self-generated. Inner Winter is a hibernation den of self reflection where you can take the societally conditioned armor off, so that you can feel the heartbeat of the Universe pulsing within you. It is the space where you remember you have always been safe, protected, and held. This fosters an unwavering sense of trust.

There is a nuance here to Inner Winter, though. We engage in the alchemical practices of nervous system regulation (which we'll explore further in this cycle) *only* when we actually are safe. During that dark night in 2012 when my protective systems were online, engaged to support me to fight, freeze, fawn or fight, would *not* have been the time to do inner alchemy. It was a time to protect myself as my Fear was warranted, sacred and ruthless in its protection. My personal Inner Winter began that night as I initiated the tender process of greeting my shadows and nurturing myself back to life, slowly but surely.

The alchemy of Inner Winter relies upon a compassionate foundation. *How gentle can you be with yourself? Are you able to activate the part of you that is able to see your own innocence, as a child of this Universe learning how to live with an open heart and grounded feet?* There is no room for shame here, as this is not how we heal. Instead, compassionate understanding, patience and trust create the alchemical potion for healing.

WHAT IS INNER WINTER?

"Hope is being able to see that there is light despite all of the darkness."
- Desmond Tutu

The literal season of winter is categorized by short days and longer nights, both of which are recognized by lower temperatures. For most life on Earth, survival isn't necessarily easy. Animals like skunks and bears are able to survive harsh winters due to hibernation, conserving energy as they drift in and out of prolonged dream-sleep states, trusting they are safe within their dens. In places where temperatures and life-giving sunshine drop, life becomes precariously beautiful. Why would our inner experience be anything different?

Just as the sun sits heavy in the sky, our inner energy is also at its lowest in Inner Winter, initiating an invitation to rest. It is a natural time to turn inward towards the Self and introspect as the desire to be social decreases, just like the waning daylight. When we give permission to be in the phase of Inner Winter, slowing down enough to rest, introspect and nourish ourselves, we open up a portal to access this season's gifts of inner safety, trust, courage and an ability to source comfort within life's mysteries.

Every inner Season that we encounter along the path of *The Akashic Alchemist* is ruled by a specific Emotion which arises to teach you more about yourself. In the season of darkness, the primary Emotion is Fear. Hardwired for survival, you have internal biological systems within you – which are automatic and below the level of your conscious awareness – that are designed to prioritize your safety above all else. Inside of you there are inherent protective mechanisms that have been conditioned since you were in the womb to identify either feelings of safety and connection or feelings of danger and threat.

Living in a fast-paced society that values output and judges the miracle of slowness as lazy, it makes sense why so many of us struggle during the literal season of winter when we are asked by Mother Nature to slow down. When this phase of life invites you into a state of self reflection and your nervous system is dysregulated, you may unconsciously seek external safety through keeping busy, distracted from having to feel the unprocessed Fear from the seasons before that rests underneath your conscious awareness.

It is no coincidence that so many suffer from anxiety and depression during the darkest months of the year when we have the least amount of energy to produce and the most amount of time to self reflect. It is well-known that many people suffer during winter with what Western allopathic medicine calls 'Seasonal Affective Disorder' (SAD). Perhaps the solution lies within aligning to the ancient ways of cyclical living.

In Five Element Theory, the season of darkness is ruled by the Water Element. As children of this Earth, we too flow in cycles, just like the waters of this planet do. You can think of the ocean's tides. A person who receives a menstrual cycle each month. The dance between feeling hungry and full, as the digestive waters allow your body to absorb nutrients and release waste. The Water Element represents energies that flow in cycles and beautifully symbolizes how we can experience inner states like feeling stagnant, frozen, peaceful, flowing, raging, boiling – hell, we can even feel salty!

On a symbolic level, the Water Element and Inner Winter also represent opening ourselves up to psychic/intuitive guidance. There is a certain level of intuitive awareness that opens up, only after we've received deep rest and feel spacious. When we try to hold too much, there isn't room for anything new to come in, which is like having a cluttered mind but wanting to receive more information. Inner Winter creates relaxation within the body to open you up to receive guidance. We practice regulating our nervous system during this Inner Season so that we can trust what information we're receiving.

This Season is also a natural time to transmute trauma, "thawing" energetic ice left over from painful memories. When we move at a slower, gentler pace, we can experiment with bringing up the things that have sunk deep down in conscious, measured steps to protect the nervous system. Inner Winter in many ways is like a pit stop, or a place to take notice of what has come before. It is often marked by themes of self reflection, introspection, and spontaneous self discovery. This stroll down memory lane can be a tender time, which is why we want to alchemize the skills of compassion, inner safety and self trust first. During my inner winter of 2012, feelings of inner safety began growing from my yoga practice as I slowly spent more time in and with my physical body.

The alchemy of Inner Winter includes engaging in practices that regulate your nervous system. If we have a dysregulated nervous system and are going deep sea diving into the cavern of our past, it can be a retraumatizing journey, and so we want to take things slow and intentional, guided by the capacity of the nervous system.

One of my teachers, Sri Mati says, "*there is nothing more powerful than a person that knows themself.*" I think this quote sums up the internal process of Inner Winter quite perfectly, as when you are in your Inner Winter you can't help but reflect on all the different parts of you. It's as if the inner current sucks you down into the very depths of your subconscious, diving for emotions that have been buried. During this Season you traverse the crevasses of your subconscious, which is an inherently brave and courageous journey.

In many ways your Inner Winter is like stepping into this obsidian cave – a sacred and internal temple site where we do shadow work. When we're resting in the obsidian cave, it's like gazing into the surface of a still lake, except you are only able to see your own reflection staring back at you. If we can sit with – and over time befriend – our own reflection and the myriad of qualities we see mirrored back to us, we can process anything life sends our way. At times intense, this season teaches us how to stay open during times of perceived constriction, which over time increases our capacity to handle stress and the fluctuations of life.

In short and in summary, Inner Winter is the season of learning how to inner resource safety and build self trust so that you can explore the memories that live within your body and foster a relationship with your intuitive body. Ruled by the Water Element – the first element that all the others manifest from – Inner Winter is a place where we explore our past, daydream about our future and raise our capacity to navigate whatever the present moment has in store.

SEASON	EMOTION	ELEMENT	GIFTS	INNER ALCHEMY
Inner Winter	Fear	Water	Trust, Memory, Intuition	Nervous System Regulation

GIFTS OF INNER WINTER

When you're navigating a Fearful time in life, consider engaging with the Inner Alchemy practices of Inner Winter. We will explore more about some of these practices in the chapter *Alchemy of Inner Winter*.

- Resourcing safety from within
- Trusting others/trusting the universe
- Positive relationship with rest
- Memory
- Inner knowing/strong intuitive connection
- Intuitive and able to dream
- Peace that arises from stillness
- Ability to allow what is
- Courageous (fearful but doing it anyway)
- Curious about the mystery of life
- Persistence
- Resourcefulness

THE MAGICK OF WATER

*"Water has a memory and carries within it our thoughts and prayers.
As you yourself are water, no matter where you are, your prayers will
be carried to the rest of the world."*
- Dr. Masaru Emoto

Inner Winter is symbolically ruled by the Element of Water -- one of the most precious resources on Earth. Without it, life as we know it couldn't survive. This fundamental element arrived on our molten planet during the early stages of the birth of our solar system, being propelled to our terrestrial home by chance when Jupiter was once unstable in its orbit. The giant gas planet was barrelling through the asteroid belt, flinging cosmic rocks all over the place. Catapulting asteroids filled with water trapped inside towards our planet, the elemental building blocks for life finally entered Earth's fiery ecosystem. The potential for liquid Water, in the form of hydrogen, became buried deep underground after more solar debris rained down on our planet.

Eventually, the pressures of Earth's molten core

became so hot that She exploded magma and minerals everywhere, releasing the hidden hydrogen – a building block for liquid Water – out and up onto the surface, intermingling with the world above. Over eons this hydrogen began to combine with oxygen, rising up as water vapor which formed massive clouds. At one point in Earth's history, Her clouds rained for thousands of years, birthing Her oceans and transforming Herself from a Fire Goddess into a Water world.

Many Indigenous, Earth-based cultures believe that Water is the Element which holds memory and carries consciousness. The Māori peoples of New Zealand and the Desana of the Amazon Basin are some of the myriad of Indigenous cultures that work with Water in a sacred way. Through drumming, intention setting and prayer, Water has been respectfully used in rituals for eons. Considered the primordial element of the universe, thousands of tribal groups across the globe have understood that Water – when paired with loving intention and gratitude – has the power to heal any ailment and amplify any positive vision for the future of oneself, and for humanity.

If you think about it, every embryo and seed begins its growth in Water. From the womb to the seed pod, these tiny Water worlds hold massive encoding for life. In our ceaseless search for other sentient life within our universe, we look for Water as we believe nothing can survive without it. In our modern colonized world many of us have been severed from our Indigenous and ancestural connection to Water. Modern science is just barely catching up to Water's ancient ability to carry memory, knowledge, wisdom and power to create change.

Japanese physician Dr. Masaru Emoto produced one of the most groundbreaking studies showing how Water is living intelligence, able to respond to human thought, intention and prayer. He introduced Water to various stimuli such as photographs, music, spoken words and mental thoughts, then flash-froze the Water to look at its microscopic crystalline structures. The results were astounding. Water that had been exposed to hate speech, erratic/discordant music or harmful thoughts produced irregular crystal patterns that did not resemble harmonic sacred geometry. On the contrary, Water that received positive affirmations, harmonic frequencies, beautiful images and mental thoughts that were in alignment with positive states like love produced stunning geometric patterns. His research even showed how polluted Water from the Fujiwara Dam was able to restore its healthy crystalline structure after a one hour prayer facilitated by the chief priest of Jyuhouin Temple, Reverend Kato Hoki.[1]

Adding to the research of Dr. Emoto is the work of Dr. Gerald Pollack, a PhD professor of bioengineering at Washington State University. It is well known that Water can take the form of solid, liquid and gas, and Dr. Pollack's research took the classification of Water to an entirely new level. He revealed the 4th state of water: slightly viscous plasma.[2] In its most highly structured state (meaning in its purest form), Water – on a microscopic level – is hexagonal in shape and slightly thicker than the Water we often drink. In this geometric form, Water is able to transmit the most amount of information – such as life-giving instructions passed between cells – in the most effective way possible. In this state, messages between cells are able to travel faster than the nervous system, which we once didn't know was possible. He showcased how most of the Water in our bodies is in this 4th state called either plasma or exclusion zone (EZ) water.[3]

Studies have shown that individual Water droplets, when placed under a microscope, produce vastly different patterns and can hold terabytes worth of historical data. Water droplets that were taken from a mine in Beijing look entirely different from holy water from a church in Italy. Even when analyzing Water droplets from a single source, we find that every single droplet carries its own unique pattern, as no two droplets are exactly the same, even in the same body of Water, as they may have traveled from other places like rain clouds or rivers. Carrying the codes of memory in the form of geometric patterns, we can see where that droplet has traveled from in its past, before it reached its current resting place. Nothing can pass through Water without leaving behind information. We will explore how to work with the memory stored in the Water of your body (your subconscious) in *Alchemy of Inner Winter.*

WHAT IF FEAR BECAME YOUR TEACHER?

"The greatest thing then, in all education, is to make our nervous system our ally as opposed to our enemy."
- William James

We've been collectively programmed to subdue ancient emotional teachers like Fear (and its symptom of anxiety) because they are uncomfortable. Regardless of how uncomfortable it felt, Fear was the most loving, protective life force coursing through my veins that fateful night in 2012. Blood pumping straight to my heart, ready for anything, it was the protective measure that empowered me to defend my life, generating a will power to survive like no other. Fear was my body's subconscious way of persevering, saying, *"yes, I want to live and I'll do anything to make it happen."* Fear is what kept me alive.

Fear only becomes a real problem when our bodies do not recognize that the danger has passed, which can happen after traumatic events when our nervous system becomes dysregulated. Even if the mind consciously recognizes that we are okay, the body does not understand our thoughts. The body has to come to believe this itself, on an energetic/emotional level. This is why repatterning the Memory of our body is so important.

If our bodies get used to living in chronic stress states and we have an imbalance of the Water Element, we can manifest a myriad of health complications like gastrointestinal issues, adrenal fatigue, autoimmune disorders, hair loss, reproductive issues and more. There is a significant need for managing Fear in a supportive way for our longevity and quality of life.

The physical manifestations of Fear (such as the symptoms of anxiety) are not punishments or our bodies attacking us. It is the miraculous body wanting to communicate to us how we're feeling. Fear is the most ancient and primal Emotion biologically evolving first as a mechanism to keep us alive. At its core, Fear is our greatest protection mechanism, born out of its love for our survival.

When we encounter moments in life that feel too much, too fast for the autonomic nervous system – which is the unconscious and automatic part of you that processes Fear – this is known as experiencing trauma. Trauma is when your biological systems identified a threat to your safety and initiated the process of either aggression/action (sympathetic nervous system activation) or disassociation and numbness (dorsal vagal activation) in order to protect you.

Trauma and prolonged exposure to stress affect your body's ability to discern if something would create connection (safety) or if it is a threat to your survival (fear). As Deb Dana, author of *Polyvagal Theory in Therapy* writes, "[t]rauma compromises our ability to engage with others by replacing patterns of connection with patterns of protection."[1]

When these wires get crossed for a significant period of

time, we begin seeing the world as a scary place. We may later identify with having anxiety. Anxiety is a symptom of underlying and unaddressed Fears that have built up in the body over time, showing us that the nervous system is living in a perpetual state of protection. It is a physical manifestation, alerting your mind to how your body is feeling.

When I'm working with my coaching clients, the first phase I take them through in my signature 3 month mentorship program is that of Inner Winter. This is our starting place for our work together so that they can learn alchemical tools for inner resourcing safety. Inner resourcing safety is when you strengthen your nervous system capacity and move into what is called regulation. Regulation means you are able to skillfully and flexibly be able to adapt to life's stressors and fluctuating states. You are able to be in flow with life.

The reason why my clients begin in Inner Winter is because it is impossible to build anything meaningful and expansive without the foundation of a regulated nervous system. Your nervous system is the primary feedback loop system that informs *how* you're feeling. Your autonomic nervous system does not communicate through language, but rather impulses and sensations that course through your bloodstream and organs. Essentially, if your nervous system is feeling unsafe, you cannot think your way out of it. You will continue to view anything that takes you out of your comfort zone as monumentally scary, which is a huge barrier when we're looking to expand, grow and evolve. Your body has to come to *believe* that you will be safe when you venture out of your hibernation den and into the wide world on its own through a process called repatterning.

Repatterning is the process of changing your autonomic nervous system's patterns of defense and protection, so that they remain on when they need to (like when in reasonable danger) and these same loving protective mechanisms that are designed to keep you alive appropriately shut *off* when they are not needed (like when you are wanting to connect deeper in intimate relationships, for example.)

When regulating your nervous system in Inner Winter, it is most important to activate your compassion muscle for the part of you that is feeling afraid. We often vilify Fear and anxiety, shaming this part of self because it is uncomfortable. From a very primal and biological standpoint, Fear is coming from an ancient and innate part of you that loves you so much, that want to see you stay alive and keep going. When we frame our Fear as arising from a loving, biologically hardwired place, we can soften the edges of self judgment.

TRAUMA THAT AFFECTS FEAR RESPONSES

Below is a brief list of various traumas that could impact the development of Water Element, namely the nervous system, affecting harmonization of Fear responses.

- Physical, emotional or sexual abuse
- Any type of childhood trauma
- Continued nervous system dysregulation
- Birth trauma
- Medical procedures
- Life threatening illness, diagnoses
- Bullying/harassment
- Early exposure to violence/abuse/death

PHYSICAL, MENTAL AND EMOTIONAL MANIFESTATIONS

Below is a brief list of physical, mental and emotional issues that can manifest from a dysregulated nervous system. In many Indigenous and ancient cultures, and within the path of *The Akashic Alchemist*, we believe that no diagnosis is permanent. When we view the body as connected to our emotions, we can transform our body through our emotional health.

- Kidney/urinary bladder issues
- Adrenal issues
- Dysregulated nervous system
- Problems with legs/ankles/knees
- Pelvic floor/reproductive issues
- Chronic ear infections/ear issues
- Bone/teeth/hair issues
- Waiting for the other shoe to drop
- Overly controlling, cautious or protective
- Difficulty trusting self/the world
- Paralyzed by Fear
- Disassociation
- Resisting Rest
- Depression
- Ruthless Drive for External Power
- Fearless/Reckless
- Grandiose God Complex
- Seasonal Affective Disorder (SAD)
- Attention Deficit Disorder (ADHD)
- Post Traumatic Stress Disorder (PTSD)
- Obsessive Compulsive Disorder (OCD)
- Anxiety/mood disorders
- Phobias
- Paranoia

Note: *This list is inspired by Traditional Chinese Medicine, Ayurveda and Tantrik Yoga Philosophy.*

PRACTICES THAT ALCHEMIZE FEAR

- Nervous system regulation/inner resourcing safety
- Breathwork
- Hypnotherapy

- Embodiment
- Shadow work
- Yoga
- Ecstatic dance
- Yoga nidra (psychic sleep)
- Somatic Release Exercises
- Trauma and Tension Release Exercises (TRE®)

"Don't think the garden loses its ecstasy in winter. It's quiet, but the roots down there are riotous."
- Rumi

Even when the Earth appears to be resting, there is so much alchemical magick happening beneath the surface, underneath the veil of our perception above ground, enabling life to flourish come spring. Resilient buds that burst into vibrant blossoms in the spring only have the energy to bloom after going dormant in winter, after all. A metaphor for us I think, that even when we rest, our bodies' mysterious intelligence is doing so much to provide us with replenishing life force beneath the surface of our conscious awareness.

Our symbolic Inner Winter represents the season of life when we are exploring the mysterious, subterranean realm of our subconscious. This is the time when you are traversing life experiences and memories that were repressed, bringing up the hidden depths of your lived experiences to be held in the light. When you enter this

Shadow realm with a compassionate understanding of the nervous system – notably that this is a biologically programmed part of you that is always trying to keep you safe – you can consciously explore your Shadow in a supportive way. You can learn what protective mechanisms you've created from your past and discern if they're still supportive, choosing whether or not you wish to keep them or repattern them.

The primary Emotion of this Inner Season is Fear, which lives in the "Water" of your body. Water represents your subconscious, your nervous system and your fascial matrix. Fear is not our enemy, but one of the most loving parts of your ancient brain, nervous system and body, that comes online to protect you. When we see this biologically supportive Emotion as our Teacher, we can become a student of its lessons. The soul lesson we can learn during this season is how to transmute Fear into Trust. Trust unfolds the more you regulate your nervous system and expand your capacity to hold life in its many flavors, textures and shapes.

Trust is a fundamental building block to move from surviving to thriving and is a gift that manifests from feeling safe. Inner resourcing safety is the fertile ground from which all of life's gifts unfurl. Once you feel safe, you rebuild your sense of trust with yourself and the world. As we explored, we cannot trick the body into feeling safe or believing that an old threat has passed. The body has to come to believe this on its own. This is where the alchemical practices we will learn about in a moment come into play.

Inner Winter is ruled by the Water Element which is able to take many forms like boiling, raging, flowing, meandering, still, stagnant and freezing. Water is a shapeshifter, just as your emotional self is. When we turn to nature – who is our greatest teacher, because we ourselves are nature – we see that sustainability comes from each cycle having a place in the grand picture. When you rest, gather reserves and create space to self reflect, you aren't lazy or slowing your progress. You are creating sustainability for what lies ahead. Rest, which you can enjoy through any practices that regulate your nervous system – increases your capacity to hold life with more ease.

When you engage with Inner Winter's Emotional Teacher of Fear and explore this Season's alchemical practices, you are able to receive the gifts of this season, namely: Memory, Trust and Intuition.

MEMORY

Modern science is just barely catching up to this ancient knowledge: Water is Consciousness and holds Memory. You are holding all of the memories of your lifetime inside of your body. This is what is known as your subconscious. Your subconscious mind isn't actually in your brain or a "mind" in the traditional sense, but is threaded through your entire body. This part of you communicates to your cognitive mind via your nervous system and your fascia. How you feel on a regular basis tells you a lot about the memories that are living in your subconscious.

The memories that are stored here are not cognitive memories. Instead, what is stored in your body are feelings. You may have unresolved and old feelings of Fear memorialized in your hips or hamstrings. You may have Anger taking up residence in your jaw. Perhaps your Grief is living in your lungs. Because the most loving and protective parts of you didn't want you to get hurt like you may have been in the past, your body took energetic "screenshots" of these memories and stored them in certain places of your body, so that you could react appropriately as needed, if your body felt the threat had returned. For example, chronic hip pain often comes from subconscious somatic memories of feeling stuck, unable to flee, or unable to find safety, such as in traumatic experiences. Your body may have spent energy preparing to find safety (such as sending blood flow and chemicals to the legs to get ready to flee). If escaping wasn't possible, it stored that memory in the hips. The body stores this memory here so that the next time you may be in a similar situation and feeling unsafe, the energy that it requires your legs to run can more effectively come back "online," reminding your conscious mind to get away.

At some point in your life it was helpful for you to hold these memories here and in this example, the chronic pain that lives here is showing up out of loving protection. Your body believes it is helping you by storing emotions in your body, so you are prepared. When we do alchemical practices like embodiment, we create time to properly feel what's been stored away in our body's memory bank so we're not living in a constant state of preparation, waiting for the other shoe to drop. With the example of chronic pain in the hips, this could look like taking some deep breaths and coming into a relaxed state, then giving yourself time to process any unresolved feelings from the past. You could then repattern those memories with more supportive ones, such as reminding the hips that they are safe and free to come and go as they please now, focusing on the safety that's being generated in the present moment.

As an embodiment coach, this is a lot of what I teach my clients who are enrolled in my mentorship programs. I guide my clients through somatic practices that create a container for them to revisit the memories of the past in a safe and mindful way. In their online course portal, clients have embodiment practices and hypnotherapy journeys to do this. Embodiment practices are guided moving meditations designed at processing unresolved memories in the body so that they can be flushed away in the bloodstream. Another alchemical practice that rewires the memories stored in your body is hypnotherapy. This is a form of guided meditation using a trance (or relaxation) state, and has the power to repattern old, outdated protective mechanisms for newer, more supportive ones. These two tools: embodiment and hypnotherapy are powerful ways to rewire old limiting beliefs, reduce pain/tension in the body and establish new, supportive beliefs.

I see many clients who have felt stagnant in talk therapy or other mental modalities of healing because they realized they couldn't think their way out of their Fear and anxiety. They had to feel it, allowing their body to come to believe that they are safe, and empowered. Nothing is ever set in stone, even the past. The memories that we hold in our body can be transmuted into more supportive versions. Clients often report that they feel rejuvenated and lighter after doing these practices.

ALCHEMICAL PRACTICE FOR MEMORY: HYPNOTHERAPY

Hypnotherapy is an amazing way to reprogram outdated beliefs & foster trust, because the practice includes nervous system regulation techniques like body scanning, breathwork and present moment awareness, which are all ways to reduce stress.

- Identify a pattern/outdated belief that you want to repattern, such as, "*I don't trust myself.*"
- Then, identify what you want the new belief to be, like "*I trust myself and feel safe in the world.*"
- If you'd like to try hypnotherapy, head to the book's website for a gifted hypnotherapy meditation to support you in reprogramming an outdated belief.

TRUST

Alchemizing Fear into Trust is a steady and measured practice of catching your nervous system up to speed with your current reality. Our biological systems are hardwired to focus on the energetic moments when you feel stress out of protection to avoid such states again. This history, stored in your subconscious, filters your reality. Establishing trust is reclaiming your right to experience life as new, no longer ruled by outdated subconscious beliefs. When we're alchemizing Fear into Trust, we can do any type of practice that expands the nervous system's capacity to handle stress.

The main practice is reminding yourself that you are safe while doing things that take you out of your comfort zone.

ALCHEMICAL PRACTICE FOR TRUST: EXPAND YOUR CAPACITY FOR STRESS

- For one week, commit to doing 1 thing that is outside of your comfort zone every day. An example would be taking a cold shower for 1

minute, focusing on taking slow and deep
breaths.
- Each time you do something outside of your
  comfort zone, you're expanding your capacity
  to handle stress. Remind yourself when doing
  these activities that you are safe and in control
  of how you feel.

Note: *If you find yourself in an unsafe environment, it is not
time to do alchemy around Trust, it is time to find physical safety.*

INTUITION

Your intuition communicates to you through the felt-sense
of your body through impulses and emotional feelings. As
they say, things can either "feel" right or "feel" wrong. In
order to learn the body's intuitive language, it is helpful to
inner resource safety, trust and rewire outdated memories
that are in the subconscious so old feelings don't drown out
the present moment awareness. Once we feel safe in the
body and build a relationship with self trust, we no longer
doubt our intuition. Intuition often comes through when
we can prioritize rest and slowness.

ALCHEMICAL PRACTICE FOR INTUITION:
MINDFUL REST

Mindful does not mean sleeping, as sleeping is a basic
biological need. Mindful rest means creating space to do
nothing. Lie outside on a blanket. Sit in the sun. Watch the
wind blow through the trees. Allow your awareness to float
from moment to moment with no agenda. No need to
meditate. No need to breathe in a particular way. Simply
rest.

Many of us struggle with rest and see it as being lazy. If so, we miss out on the wisdom that can only come through when we rest. Spring requires the energy that is saved during dormant winter. Your future blossoming needs your soft and gentle rest in Inner Winter. Even when you rest, your body is hard at work. Maybe that will inspire you to rest easy!

ALCHEMICAL TOOLS FOR INNER WINTER

- Nervous system regulation
- Inner resourcing safety
- Building Self Trust
- Hypnotherapy
- Embodiment
- Breathwork
- Shadow Work
- Somatic/Emotional Release Exercises
- Yoga Nidra (Psychic Sleep)
- Journaling
- Yoga
- Emotional Freedom Technique (EFT)
- Light Physical Exercise
- Swimming
- Spending Time In Nature

CYCLE TWO: INNER SPRING

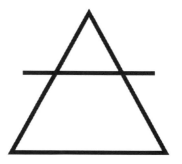

THERE IS A PART OF YOU THAT KNOWS

Your thoughts and words are spells,
paving the path that is laid out in front of you.

The moment you know of as Now
is the culmination of all that has been spoken before.

Remember: your mind is not your enemy.

Your mind is the architect,
waiting for clear instructions.

It is up to you to direct this creative project,
paving the path that you know of
as your life.

Remember: your words are spells.

INNER SPRING AT A GLANCE

PRIMARY ELEMENT
Wood/Air

PRIMARY EMOTION
Anger Spectrum

RELATED CHAKRA
Throat (Vishuddha)

GIFTS OF THE SEASON
Clarity and decision making
Creativity
Resolve to stick with intentions
Resiliency
Planning
Organizing
Will to become
Enjoying the journey
Imagination
Having direction
Hopes and dreams
Inventiveness
Flexibility and adaptability

**DIVINE FEMININE SHADOW OF
ANGER**
Shaming
Feeling guilty
Loud inner critic

**DIVINE FEMININE SHADOW OF
ANGER**
Stuck in duality (good/bad -
right/wrong)
Self-sabotage
'Shoulding' on oneself

**DIVINE MASCULINE SHADOW
OF ANGER**
Violence
Blame
Passive Aggression
Bullying
'Shoulding' on others

PHYSICAL ISSUES
Allergies
Liver/Gallbladder Issues
Tendon/Ligament/Nail Issues
Headaches
Chronic Jaw Tension
Menstrual Pain/Disorders
Blood Disorders/Issues
Eye Issues

TRAUMA
Shaming, constant criticism
Any type of abuse

INNER SPRING AT A GLANCE

TRAUMA
Abandonment, rejection or loss
Betrayal
Intuition is invalidated
Exposure to frightening
environments (war, emergency
personnel, etc.)
Religious/Spiritual abuse
Misinformation, lies
Continuously invalidated
Stifling education
Information continuously withheld

ALCHEMY PRACTICES
Setting Intentions + Following
Through
Physical Exercise
Keeping an organized planner
Doing what brings you pleasure
Tracking patterns (tests, triggers)
Anger Release Exercises
Embodiment
Journaling/Affirmations
Yoga

AFFIRMATIONS
I am the alchemist of my life.
The information I need comes to
me at the perfect time.
I am open to learning.
I don't need to know all of the
answers.
I am capable of following through.

"Creativity is intelligence having fun."
- Albert Einstein

After scheduling all of my classes I began looking for apartments, apprehensively preparing for this next chapter of my life. My relationship of 4 years was cracking at the seams, I was considering keeping a job that didn't fulfill me so I could make ends meet during grad school and was getting ready to move to Queens. After looking at tiny closets they only call apartments within the boroughs of New York City, I was on the verge of an emotional breakdown as I came to terms with life not panning out as I'd hoped.

Two weeks after my long-distance relationship ended, I was checking my spam folders on my email account to keep track of financial aid communications from my university. Scrolling through hundreds of unseen and unopened emails to find the appropriate communications, a particular subject header caught my attention. '*Do you want to study abroad for your master's program?*' the email header read. Why, yes. I didn't know I wanted to, but now that you mention it…

Two months later, instead of packing my life up to live in Queens, I was preparing for a trip of a lifetime. Deciding to follow a thread of aliveness – despite feeling unsure if it was the right choice – I was now enrolled in a study abroad Master's program where I could live overseas and study internationally, moving countries every semester. It was an opportunity I didn't have to work to find, but had to strive to make a reality.

A few days before I was scheduled to depart for Bangkok and move my life on the road for a year, I threw myself a going away party down the shore. After an evening of dancing in Atlantic City, the fun came with a few…repercussions. The following morning crowned itself as the reigning champion of the worst hangover of my life. Dehydrated and making it only a few steps outside of the bathroom threshold just after waking, I fainted. Unfortunately I was holding a ceramic mug which shattered as I fell face first into it. I woke up moments later covered in blood with the entire house of guests surrounding me in a panic. Seeing horrified faces looking back at me when I lifted up my head, I knew by their facial expressions that I was not in a great way. My face had broken my fall as I collapsed head first into the cup, then into the floor beneath it.

After many hours of waiting in the emergency room, I learned that I broke my nose, fractured my cheek, split open my eyebrow, had double black eyes and needed countless stitches, not to mention the epic concussion. All of this unfolded within forty-eight hours before I was due to depart for Southeast Asia.

Just the week prior and previous to my injuries, my greatest worry was sorting out how I was going to pack my entire life into two suitcases for a year. Procrastinator at heart, I had never regretted saving my packing until the last minute as I did that day. In tremendous pain and loaded with a foggy concussion, I pondered how in the fuck I was supposed to pack up my entire life in my condition. As I conquered one obstacle, another one reared its head, like the whack a mole game that I loved playing as a kid, except this time, the game was much less fun.

As my mom used her discernment to sort out what to pack for me, I realized that I had forgotten that one very important piece of documentation was not on me. My student visa which allowed me to enter and study in Bangkok for two months during the semester abroad was inside my passport. The document in question was still in New York City at the Thai Embassy, dropped off eight weeks ago for processing.

Like a true Italian mother, my mom expressed her worry for me 'burning the candle at both ends' and questioned whether this was all a sign whether or not I should stay home. After that brief moment of considering throwing in the towel passed, my dad hopped in the car, going on a rescue mission for my passport. All systems were go in my family as I lay on the struggle bus. I received a call at 3:55pm from my dad that he took the wrong exit and ended up in the Bronx instead of Brooklyn, where the embassy was. They closed at 4pm.

I called the embassy multiple times and left them just as many messages begging them not to close. That my dad was shortly going to be there and I *desperately* needed my passport as my flight was leaving at 7am the next morning, out of Philadelphia. My dad didn't arrive until 4:45pm and to all of our surprise, and through the grace of the Universe, there was a gentleman who waited outside holding my passport after the embassy had closed. He had received my messages and was waiting for him for almost an hour.

A mere twelve hours later – miraculously with my passport in hand – I made my way to the airport, two suitcases of my life trailing behind me. Intimidated by the prospect of greeting the bigness of this world alone, I began to question what it was I was actually doing as I checked in for my flight and sat down waiting to board. Maybe all of these hiccups *were* signs to turn this struggle bus around and go home. As I was pondering my life's choices I heard my name being called over the loudspeaker and was asked to come to the service desk for my flight. They said that I had been flagged by airport security as not looking fit to travel and that I'd need to go under medical examination to see if I was medically okay to fly. At that moment, in a swell of frustration and unstoppable determination, I decided that I was going to decide the fate of my own destiny. I had the power to create any reality I desire. I was getting on that fucking plane.

When asked how I was doing by the medical personnel I kindly, clearly spoke to the woman giving me my examination that I was not about to turn back now. Over-sharing with her as per usual, I opened up about how it had taken me so much to get here and I had to follow through with my mission. She continued to question me in a movie-type-of-way: *do you know what year it is? Who is the president? What is your full name?* I answered all of her questions with flying colors. Whatever signs of life she was looking for when she shined that mini flashlight in my eyes were present and she let me board that one-way plane.

The year that followed wound up being one of the biggest initiations of my life. I explored the loneliest corners of my mind late at night in many foreign countries.

Every semester I packed my life up again to prepare for being the new kid at school, wondering if I'd be able to conjure the energy to reintroduce myself and nurture new relationships. It was as if every semester I destroyed the older version of me that came before, devouring her to rebirth a new me. I learned more about myself in those eleven months as I studied in five countries and backpacked in eleven more.

What I've found is that when I set out to manifest big, bold visions, I usually am met with unexpected hurdles that keep me on my toes, strengthening my resolve and fostering an unwavering commitment to my vision. It's almost as if the Universe is testing me so that I'm ready for the next phase of expansion. It is a beautiful spiral dance of co-creation between me and my Higher Self. It's like Great Spirit would knock on my door saying, *hey, I know you prayed for this. I'm here to help you get ready for it.*

These days I find comfort in believing that the Universe's tests are not something I can fail, because regardless of the outcome, I am evolving. In a way, these obstacles are initiations to prepare for the life upgrade. That arduous trek from Atlantic City to Philadelphia, all to get my ass in a Bangkok classroom seat was just the beginning of my journey. In the past it would have been easy to misjudge the hurdles as signs to give up, but now I see setbacks as a subtle encouragement to stay focused on my target. Sometimes, life is not easy. We do not always manifest what we want delivered on our doorstep on a butterfly with a rainbow trail.

Sometimes, we gotta keep our eyes focused on what we want, remain in our self worth, and if it's meant for us, we are sure to make our mark.

WHAT IS INNER SPRING?

"All things human change."
- Alfred Lord Tennyson

If Inner Winter is the warm womb of subconscious exploration where we have space to rest, reflect and dream, Inner Spring is when we leave the den of hibernation and begin getting organized, mapping out our next move. Without this Divine Masculine energy of planning, nothing would get done. We'd simply remain adrift in the sea of Divine Feminine emotion, going with the unconscious flow and seeing where the current takes us, or remaining cloaked under the veil of our Fears. There is a Season for feeling our feels and healing our trauma, just as there comes a time to set intentions and make a plan for our next level of expansion.

Inspired by Five Element Theory, Inner Spring is ruled by the element of Wood and represents the quality of resiliency. Have you ever seen those photos of trees bursting out of the top of city gutters, determined to find the light? How about grass that relentlessly sprouts up between the cracks in the pavement? That's the energy of your Inner Spring: clear, flexible and focused intention that is innovative and resilient. When nature has a plan, no obstacle can get in its way. It is a frequency of evolution that says *I can figure this out.* Your Inner Spring invites you to remain rooted in upward growth, just like the tree that unabashedly finds the light, no matter what. Your soul has the same technology.

When we set intentions and adventure out of the hibernation den, we will inevitably stumble across obstacles. I find that the epic journey of Frodo Baggins in The Lord of The Rings is the perfect metaphor for this season. He and his companions continuously met with the unexpected but they never gave up on their vision of restoring harmony back to their world.

You have probably found yourself on the same struggle bus that myself, Mr. Baggins and his comrades were on. Think of a time in your life where you were gaining momentum, catching a groove and moving towards embodied clarity. You could tell you were finally headed to where you wanted to be. And then it happened. The Great Interruption. Whether it be getting sick, injured, fired, broken up with, waking up wildly hungover, feeling triggered or simply surprised by the sheer audacity of life throwing a curveball into the mix of your currently well-maintained process, Inner Spring is the Season of hitting a hurdle. This Inner Season may include words like *are you fucking kidding me* more than any other.

Naturally, our Emotional Teacher during this phase is Anger, which exists on a spectrum. From annoyance to sacred fucking rage, it encompasses any of the words that express your discontentment with what is happening in your present reality. The invitation during this season is to learn from your Anger, just as you did with your Fear, to receive the wisdom of this Emotion. The gifts that unfold when Anger is alchemized are motivation, direction and focused intention.

SEASON	EMOTION	ELEMENT	GIFTS	INNER ALCHEMY
Inner Spring	Anger	Wood	Motivation, Direction + Focused Intention	Transmute Anger into Aligned Action

GIFTS OF INNER SPRING

When Anger bubbles up to the surface, consider engaging with the alchemy practices of Spring. We will explore more about some of these practices in the chapter *Alchemy of Inner Spring*.

- Resolve to stick with intentions
- Clarity and decision making
- Creativity
- Resiliency
- Planning
- Organizing
- Will to become
- Enjoying the journey
- Imagination
- Having direction
- Hopes and dreams
- Inventiveness
- Flexibility and adaptability
- Positive Self Talk

THE MAGICK OF WOOD

"Our bodies know they belong; it is our minds that make our lives so homeless."
- John O'Donohue

Being first generation Dominican-American on my father's side, for many reasons I grew up with a different childhood than many of my peers. Living in a predominantly white, middle-class suburban town, I didn't have any friend's parents that spoke to their plants like my dad does. In our household, we believe that plants are always communicating with us, that they are more intelligent than we could imagine. I realize now that this wisdom my dad passed on to me was keeping our Indigenous Taino and African ancestry alive, whether we had the words to recognize it or not.

One day in early Spring, as the idea of this book was gestating, I noticed how the Maples that lined my street were the first to courageously bloom their vibrant flowers and witnessed how later they were the first to drop their seeds. That Spring they taught me a little bit more about being a trailblazer. As I sat beneath a massive Grandmother Maple tree, proudly perched along the lakeshore in my neighborhood, I asked her about her life. "*How did you know, before you became a tree, which way was up? When you were just a little seed, shaped like a helicopter, how did you know which direction to grow to find the sun,*" I curiously asked.

"*There is a divine intelligence woven into all things, including you. You always know which way is up. You simply have to feel it and tell yourself it is so. Most importantly, you have to trust that you know,*" she replied.

In Robin Kimmerer's legendary book, *Braiding Sweetgrass,* she dedicates an entire chapter to the Maples. Robin taught me that the Onondaga people consider them the leader of the trees.[1] They are the first to provide a nutritional gift to us, in the form of maple syrup, after the long slumber of Winter. These leaders of the trees even have a New Moon named after them: *Zisbakwtoke Gises* - The Maple Sugar Moon, which lands in either February or March, just as the maple sap begins to rise in their trunks from the warming of the soil.[2]

As I learned more about the Maples, I became enthralled by the trees around me, eager to learn more about their life cycle. Inspired by Kimmerer's background as an ethnobotanist, I wanted to know more about how seeds find their way to the sun. Grandmother Maple taught me much, and I knew there had to be science behind it. I turned to the best place I know to find such information: trusty Google.

How do seeds know which way is up, despite being buried underground? Google confirmed the channeled wisdom from Grandmother Maple: every seed comes equipped with technology to be able to detect which way is up. They do so by sensing Earth's gravity.[3] Although scientists do not know yet exactly how this happens, seeds can feel which way is down (the direction to grow roots) and which way is up (the direction to sprout to find the sun), based on the tug of the Earth. It may take them a few tries, but they always figure it out. This is a beautiful metaphor for Spring. When we're paying attention, we're always receiving subtle tugs towards the most optimal direction to go in life, and if we happen to stumble or get turned around, the internal compass of universal intelligence will always right your way.

Conceptually, trees are the closest to the symbolism of the Wood Element. Upward in nature, Wood energy rises, just like the maple sap in late Winter and early Spring. This archetypal upward energy represents motivation, resiliency and an ability to change. Wood energy of Spring follows Water of Winter, bringing us to shore so that we can head out onto the next stop in your life's journey. Otherwise, you'd be floating in the Divine Feminine ocean of Water, tenderly and introspectively feeling your feels, drifting without direction. Wood is the Divine Masculine balance that comes after the reflective time in Winter to initiate action within you.

Some schools of thought correlate Wood (of Five Element Theory) to the Wind Element (such as in Native American cultures). The Navajo people of the Four Corners (Arizona, Utah, Colorado and New Mexico) have a special and significant relationship to the Wind Element. There is said to be a specific form of wind that sits in the ear, which "*give[s] instructions, answers to questions, or predict[s] the future; [these winds] are also the reason for hanging a feather from the ear: to show that the winds are communicating with that person.*"[4] I correlate this type of archetypal Wind to the feeling of getting a divine download. A divine download is when you get a spark of an idea, seemingly out of nowhere, that supports your soul's evolution. This is called a ping. A ping is when you suddenly receive motivation to do something, no matter how small. It could be a ping nudging you to call an old friend or go out for a walk. What's important is that you listen and follow through on pings. They may very well be spiritual breadcrumbs that are leading you down a trail you have yet to know the destination of, guiding you along the mysterious path of your awakening.

When I think of Wind carrying messages, I also reflect upon how trees communicate. Many trees use the complex neural-like network of mycelium (the subterranean side of mushrooms that mimic neural networks in the brain). Some species of trees also communicate with the wind, sending messages in the form of pheromones to one another. In both forms of communication, trees communicate with one another, such as when there is danger like disease or drought. The Wind carries their distress and support signals.[5] It has been said by many Indigenous cultures, such as the Hopi of Arizona and the Mexica of central México, that Wind carries messages. Science is just catching up to this ancient wisdom.

Whether you resonate with the word Wood or Wind, the message from these archetypal Elements is similar: if plants and trees innately know how to find their way out of the darkness of soil to find the light, so do you. The trust that you cultivated during Inner Winter will support you so that you can rely on the information you're receiving as guidance. Messages from your Highest Self and Universal Source Consciousness (aka God) are being sent to you all the time, arriving as divine downloads, carried on the Wind. When you're present and paying attention, Wood/Wind is always sending you pings, guiding you towards your next destination along the path you know of as your life.

WHAT IF ANGER BECAME YOUR
TEACHER?

"Give me a place to stand and I will move the earth."
- Archimedes

On May 25th, 2020, three months into quarantine, the world watched as George Floyd was murdered by the hands of Minneapolis police, arresting him unjustly. They violently subdued and suffocated him with a knee to his neck for a staggering nine minutes and twenty-nine seconds. With the world slowed to the pace of a sloth due to COVID-19, folks who previously may have not acknowledged the injustices that happen all the time had nowhere to turn an ignorant eye to. With distractions of the hustle gone, many eyes and hearts finally opened to the centuries-long reign of systemic injustice. In a world that heartbreakingly continued business as usual each time a young Black, Brown or Indigenous youth was murdered by the hands of police, it was long overdue when the American people began voicing their outrage. This was the undercurrent of sacred rage, alive in the collective consciousness, gunning for systemic change. This sacred rage is the energy that can change the world.

At the time of writing this book, courageous women in Iran are fighting for their human rights in regards to marriage, divorce, child custody, finances and travel. In heart-opening displays of radical courage, Iranian women are letting their hair down and dancing and singing in public – all at the expense of their life – as these activities are illegal for women there and come with grave consequences. Their bravery is a response to their justified sacred rage and is inspiring mini movements all across the globe. Across the world we are seeing these collective sparks of sacred rage start wildfires, demanding change.

Right now we are undergoing a time of great crumbling of outdated systems as many people are awakening to their place in the world. Questioning whether or not we should rip up the very foundation of the systems in place and start over, we are beginning to see the societal and psychological harm that stems from living in a colonized world creeping out from the veil of the collective shadow. With the world's resources depleting, oceans rising, gas prices skyrocketing and public policies seemingly going backwards rather than feeling like progress, it is no wonder why some may feel entitled to scream at the stranger who unknowingly cuts them off on the highway.

Tension can be felt at grocery stores, in Uber rides and at gas stations. Sometimes I feel like chaos is bubbling as the collective unconscious is yearning for a world that looks and feels different, boiling the global pot. We have a global undercurrent of repressed anger, the stifling of which only exacerbates it more. Anger that goes unaddressed is like turning up the setting on a pressure cooker without opening the valve for the steam to release. We're bound to explode at some point.

Vilified and shamed, Anger and its various shades of red are considered to be innately violent or harmful, but this is only when this sacred Emotional Teacher goes unaddressed. Within the work that I teach, I consider the Emotions that flow through me as archetypal parts of me. How do you feel when you are unheard or ignored? It's no wonder why when Anger goes unaddressed, this part gets louder and louder!

When we're being initiated by Inner Spring and Anger is present, this Emotion is coming online because some part of you is saying, "*this is not what I had imagined for myself or for the world. This is not what I want.*"

Through feeling this Emotion, you gain access to one of the gifts of Inner Spring: motivation. Sometimes it is through knowing what you don't want that leads you to finding more of what you do want. Feeling your anger in a responsibly safe way allows you to communicate to deeper parts of yourself that have felt abandoned, rejected or shamed in the past. Our Anger allows us to acknowledge when we've been harmed, opening to feel the more tender emotions that rest beneath its surface. Anger is usually resting upon a deeper core wound like grief, sadness, rejection, abandonment, threats to safety, fear or unworthiness, for example. If we never treat Anger as a teacher and do not see our triggers as teachers for growth, we never get to receive the wisdom (and healing of underlying Emotions) that rests beneath it.

THE SHADES OF ANGER

In no particular order, below is a list of words that fall under the overarching word of Anger, connected to Inner Spring.

- Irritated
- Annoyed
- Frustrated
- Loathing
- Disgusted
- Enraged
- Indignant
- Impatient
- Resentful
- Bitter
- Irate
- Outraged
- Furious
- Pissed Off
- Grumpy
- Judgemental
- Heated
- Exacerbated
- Offended
- Tested
- Livid
- Sacred Fucking Rage
- Angry
- Cranky

TRAUMA THAT AFFECTS ANGER

Below is a brief list of various traumas that could impact the development of your Wood/Wind Element, which in turn affects the harmonization of Anger.

- Verbal abuse
- Constant screaming
- Authoritarian caretakers, criticism (stifling of voice)
- Abandonment, rejection or loss
- Growing up around alcoholism or substance abuse (or unable to express emotions, speak how you're feeling or feel safe to trust)
- Betrayal
- Misinformation, lies, mixed messages
- Continuously invalidated
- Stifling education
- Requirement to keep secrets (or threatened if you're honest)

PHYSICAL, EMOTIONAL AND MENTAL MANIFESTATIONS

Below is a brief list of possible physical, emotional and mental issues that can manifest from a dysregulated Wood/Wind Element.

- Allergies
- Liver/gallbladder Issues
- Tendon/ligament/nail issues
- Headaches
- Chronic jaw tension
- Menstrual pain/disorders
- Blood disorders/issues
- Eye issues
- Violence

- Bullying
- 'Shoulding' to others
- Incessant guilt
- Inner critic
- Stuck in duality (good/bad - right/wrong)
- Self sabotage
- 'Shoulding' to oneself
- Passive Aggression
- Blame

Note: *This list is inspired by Traditional East Asian Medicine, Ayurveda and Tantrik Yoga Philosophy.*

PRACTICES TO ALCHEMIZE ANGER

- Setting Intentions + Following Through
- Physical Exercise
- Keeping an organized planner
- Tracking pings/intuitive hits of guidance
- Anger Release Exercises
- Embodiment
- Yoga
- Journaling/Affirmations

"You are the living light made manifest."
- Sri Mati

Just like all of the baby seeds on planet Earth, you know how to right yourself when you get turned upside down. Embedded into your consciousness is the same intelligence that weaves itself into all life on Earth, guiding you to not only survive, but thrive. You know what direction you need to go to grow. It is not uncommon to feel unsure of what you want, or feel unsure if you're on the right path. Rest assured though – your soul knows. From the soul's perspective, you can never make a wrong choice, as all paths lead Home.

You are an active participant in your soul's plan. Once you claim your sovereignty over the direction you're headed, you're unstoppable. Every single moment you are presented with opportunities to act on that sovereignty, invited to make choices. Astonishingly, it is estimated that in a single day we can make up to 35,000 decisions![1] The potential of where your life will go can shift at any given moment, as every decision you make shifts you onto a new timeline, which is one path out of infinite possibilities. You are birthing a new reality for yourself with every yes and every no.

At any time you can say, *"enough of this!"* or, alternatively, *"more please."* Because you can change your trajectory at any given time – just like the seed that sprouted a few false starts – no time in the past was wasted. It was all valuable information that contributed to this curriculum you call your life. It's easy to get caught up in the conditioned belief that we can somehow make wrong choices. From the vantage point of your soul, every single thing that is happening, and that has happened in your life, is for the betterment of your evolution. You are the living light made manifest, meaning you are Source Consciousness learning more about the human experience through the perspective of you. Every impactful moment that was recorded in your nervous system was stored away as valuable information, teaching the living light more about itself. In essence, you are teaching you, through your life's curriculum.

The reason why you cringe when thinking back on questionable decisions you made is because you are now energetically so far away from where you were, that the vibrational difference between both versions of you is so strong you can feel it. The pang you feel when reflecting on those moments when you erred in judgment or rationale is a helpful sensation, because you can sense and feel your evolution in a tangible way. You can feel, on a somatic level, that you've grown. We are meaning making creatures, and sometimes we make these sensations mean something bigger than they are. That feeling of cringe in the body doesn't need to rot into shame; instead let it be alchemized into gratitude for how far you've come.

I used to sit awake at night and pick apart my decision making. *How could I have found myself in an abusive relationship? I thought I was smarter than that…*I lived with many regrets. At the time I did not have these tools and I felt lost at sea, drowning in shame and self doubt.

I didn't see it at the time, but all of my past experiences now feed my creative wellspring in my soul-led business. I coach women recovering from the trauma of abusive relationships or abusive childhoods. I support people in regulating their nervous system to find safety. I teach tools to repattern the subconscious so that people can experience liberation from limiting thought loops like the inner critic or self sabotage. I've created online courses on getting to know your shadow and befriending it. The inspiration behind all of these programs and offerings is my lived experience, as I can still reach out and touch, sense and feel those past versions of me who needed these tools so badly.

I create based on what I wished I had, inspired to guide people through some of their most difficult times, informed by the courage, resilience and strength I gathered during my darkest Winters and most rageful Springs. In all of my life experiences, even the ones I cringe while thinking about, I learned something. Learning is part of why I am here.

In order to remember more of why your soul came, you cannot turn outside of yourself, seeking the answers from the outside. They will not be found in a book, a certificate program or from your tarot card reader. You will not stumble upon them in a yoga teacher training or retreat. Your most trusted teachers cannot reveal the answers you seek. The Way is unique to you and only you know how to get there. If you're confused, stuck, regretting past decisions or afraid to make the next move, it is my hope that the trust you're cultivating in Inner Winter supports you in Inner Spring. The Way – *your* Way – will reveal itself more and more, with each progressive step forward, following each little ping and breadcrumb.

When you engage with Inner Spring's Emotional Teacher of Anger and explore this Season's alchemical practices, you are able to receive the gifts of this season, namely: Organization, Motivation and Intention.

ORGANIZATION

It took a little while for my nervous system to adapt and my mind to calm when I moved to Rishikesh India to study yoga for two months. India was one of the most vibrant places I had ever lived with a rambunctious heart and soul that to this day goes unmatched. During training our meditation classes were always at 5:30pm – a time when the city came alive for prayer after people were relieved from work. Just about every day there were throngs of people chanting the *Maha Mantra*, coupled with the buzzing of motos and thousands of tourists who made their pilgrimage to this sacred city. To say that things were loud – at all times, actually – would be an understatement.

We spent one hour meditating each day, which was a *significant* amount of time, as most of us were beginners. Much bubbled up to the surface during that hour time slot together between that October and November of 2014. During one particular day, perhaps a week or two into training, a frustrated fellow student asked a question I think we all were thinking: *how am I supposed to meditate when it is so damn loud!?*

My first meditation teacher, who was one of the facilitators during my 500-Hour Yoga Teacher Training, was an embodied soul who had that sparkle behind his eyes. He let your heart know he was home within his body, present with you. When this student exasperatedly asked this question, he looked at him with a smile and taught me one of the foundational lessons about meditation. Meditation is not about creating the perfect moment and unplugging from the world, but moving yourself into the world as it is. He said to watch what thoughts, frustrations and beliefs rose up to the surface – that by noticing and organizing your thoughts, you were making alchemical gold.

I learned that meditation was actually more like a volcano: the first few weeks, months, or even years is allowing the repressed, stagnant or dormant energy that's been pushed down from life's pace to rise up to the surface and spill out. He taught me that when the volcano erupts, it's better to let it than force it back down. The key here is to not just let it come up and out, but to notice what themes arise. Are you frustrated with the present moment? Thinking about certain chapters of your past? Worrying about money or time? Meditation becomes a process of organizing and categorizing the themes that arise so you can see what your subconscious is really thinking about. This is what it means to bring awareness to your thoughts. Then, you consciously choose to come back to your anchor like your breath, for example.

Our minds become cluttered from constant input, and meditation can be a practice of organizing this clutter through noticing where the mind drifts away to, and consciously returning back to the present moment *after* you acknowledge where you drifted off to. It's a powerful practice to notice what thought loops are cycling in the background of your awareness, as it can point you towards what parts of self are wanting alchemy.

ALCHEMICAL PRACTICE FOR ORGANIZATION:
MEDITATION

Mostly everything we do in our day to day lives is an acquiring practice, meaning we are absorbing more and more information at any given moment. Reading other peoples' opinions. Assessing strangers' facial expressions. Downloading other peoples' content. We're engorged by consumption. There are few things that are purifying for the soul, but meditation is one.

Meditation is single-handedly the most effective way to declutter the mind. The best part is that it is accessible to every single Soul on this planet, for free. In Inner Winter, you regulate your nervous system so that you can hold more capacity to reflect on your past and where you've been. In Inner Spring, you meditate so that you can befriend the different parts of your mind and declutter. Think: spring cleaning. You can only receive divine downloads when you have space to hold them.

Consider that your mind is like a volcano, stuffed with all of the thoughts you don't have time to think about. *Bills. Seventh grade trauma. That argument with the neighbor. What's for dinner? The song you heard at Target and now you can't get that one line out of your head.* Looping in the back of your mind, whether you're conscious of it or not, is a myriad of thoughts that, without meditation, have nowhere to go. The goal of meditation is not to clear your mind. Meditation is about becoming *aware* of what is in your mind. The first days, weeks, months and even years of a consistent meditation practice is bringing consciousness to the things you are already subconsciously thinking about. It's letting the volcano erupt for a bit. After some time of erupting, it will naturally clear on its own. There is nothing extra you need to do except set your intentions and continuously practice.

I would meditate once every few months and feel frustrated that it wasn't "working." Similarly, it's like going to the gym for one day and waking up the next, upset that I didn't turn into a bodybuilder. What I teach to my students enrolled in my Fall In Love With Meditation program is that meditation is more about consistency. Showing up every day without judging the practice as good or bad, without analyzing whether it 'worked' or not, is the ticket. In the beginning, focus on getting your minutes on the cushion and establishing a new habit. Seedlings don't judge their false starts and u-turns. They come back to their intention: to find the light – and they try again. If meditation is new to you, please go easy on yourself. There is no such thing as meditating wrong, or being bad at it!

Here are a few things I wish I knew when I was first learning about meditation that would have made my journey a lot more enjoyable and accessible:

1. **Be Consistent.** Show up every day, regardless of how you feel, and meditate around the same time to establish a habit. Routine will help your nervous system find stability in the process.

2. **Choose Something to Focus On.** I used to think that the goal of meditating is "thinking about nothing" when in reality, it's a mental organizational tool and mind-strength-training, getting stronger each time you bring yourself back to your anchor when you drift away. Set your intention to place your focus on 1 thing – this is your "anchor" to come back to when you get distracted. Your breath. Music. Gazing at a mandala. My recommendation is to begin with

doing guided meditations or guided breathwork so that the person's voice is your anchor.

3. **Start Small.** Begin meditating for three to five minutes a day. You can easily give yourself that time. When the time feels like it flies by, add on 1 minute, slowly building up your meditative "muscle" over time.

4. **Notice.** When the mind drifts away – it will – notice what you are thinking about. The past? The future? Take inventory of any limiting beliefs or thought loops. Notice – is there a common recurring theme of what you're thinking about? Avoid shaming your thinking. Do your best to notice.

5. **Return To Your Anchor.** When your mind drifts away – it will – after noticing where the mind went, guide yourself back to your anchor. Notice if you tend to judge or critique yourself for getting distracted. Practice compassion for those parts wanting to get it right.

6. **Don't Judge.** There's no such thing as a "bad meditation." You did it! One metaphorical bicep curl in the mind-building training of meditation! Celebrate.

Note #1: For some individuals, meditation during times of great stress or directly after a traumatic incident can have the opposite effect, creating anxiety. For tools on navigating those times, refer to Inner Winter which supports creating inner safety in the body rather than exploring the mind.

Note #2: The first hour after waking and the last hour before sleep are some of the most powerful times to meditate. Meditating in the morning sets the tone for your day. Meditating at night helps clear your energy. Play around with when you meditate, eventually working towards 'bookending' your practice, meaning meditating both in the morning and at night. It took me 4 years to build a consistent, daily practice. After that was established, I then added an evening meditation. It's better to start small and build sustainably.

Tools: I recommend the free app Insight Timer to establish a meditation practice. You can set timers with soft music and ending chimes or gongs. You can access thousands of incredible teachers, styles and techniques and star your favorites and see ratings and reviews from others. It's easy to find meditations that are any length of time and for any level of experience. If you'd like to meditate with me on the app, head to the book's website to access my profile and meditations. I'd love to guide you through your first practice!

MOTIVATION

Motivation happens when we're turned on by certain activities, alive with life force when we think about them. Cultivating motivation happens over time and evolves when we follow small hits of inspiration, called pings. I invite my mentorship clients to track their pings and notice what comes of them. They write down on the downloadable PDF in their online course portal any time they get such a breadcrumb, and track the date. They also have space to return back to that ping to add if anything manifested from that.

For example, one client shared that she received a ping to sing more, which then inspired her to look up some opportunities to do so online. She happened to stumble upon a singing festival that had the perfect schedule. Following the ping, she attended. When she returned home she excitedly shared how this retreat opened her heart significantly, creating meaningful relationships and connections with others, while inspiring more motivation to sing more. By keeping track of the ping, and noticing what happened when she followed through with it, the practice built up her subconscious trust muscle. She strengthened her subconscious's ability to see that these seemingly random urges were opportunities to cultivate new skills and find clearer direction on where to put her energy. Her journey was inspiring to witness, as the entire summer was spent following pings and being delighted by how much motivation she self generated.

ALCHEMICAL PRACTICE FOR MOTIVATION: TRACK YOUR PINGS

Throughout the day your Highest Self is always sending you information and guidance, and this guidance comes in the form of inspired "pings." A ping is when you feel a sudden urge to take some sort of aligned action. It may be a call to go out on a walk, call an old friend, or pull out your art supplies. Inspiration and flowing creativity unfolds naturally when we listen to pings. Tracking your pings allows you to see the miraculous ways your soul is always inspiring you! Be sure to not only track your pings, but follow through with them!

- In your journal, turn to a blank page and title it "Intuitive Pings" (or, alternatively, head to the book's website and print out the Ping PDF).
- Anytime you get a hit of inspiration that seems to come out of nowhere, write down what you were inspired to do. It could be subtle and small, or a leap of faith. It's all significant.
- Follow through with the inspired action.

- After a month, go back to your list and notice any themes. Is there some pattern emerging that your soul is nudging you towards? Writing? Creating art? Spending time outside? Be sure to check back in later with your journal to see what aligned action your soul is calling you to take.

Note: *Pings always show up as little hits of inspiration. They don't speak through anxiety, or 'should'-ing on yourself. They are instantaneous moments of guidance. Remember: there is no such thing as something too small or insignificant to jot down.*

FOCUSED INTENTION

Intentions are different from setting visions and goals or declaring resolutions, which can sometimes perpetuate shame or feelings of disappointment. What happens when you set out to do something specific and measurable and feel that you've fallen short? Instead, when you find yourself desiring to do something – like when you have a vision for your future – discern *why* it is that you want to do that thing. Do you want to be a published author? Do you want to bring in more income? Would you like to manifest your dream home? Underneath the things that you want lies an emotional meaning behind them. What would publishing a book represent? Money? A home? When you're clear on *why,* you can more easily manifest the what.

For example, let's say you want to manifest more financial wealth. What do you feel money represents to you? Freedom? Safety? Success? From there, a simple intention could be: *I am free. I am safe. I am successful.* While stating this intention, you could focus on all the ways you already have these qualities in your life. Rather than focus on what you don't have, you place your awareness on the emotional states that you want to feel more of, and embody that as much as possible in the present. This builds the subconscious muscles in a different way. For many people who are struggling with lack, if they were to set the intention of, "*I am abundant,*" or, "*I am wealthy,*" when they repeat these intentions over and over again, their subconscious may inadvertently think about how they don't have those things, which ironically creates more resistance to what they want.

Intention setting, when done mindfully, and focused on the why beneath what you want, is like going in through the back door to manifest based on emotions, rather than measurable things you can check off a list. If you'd like to learn more about the art of manifesting with intention, check out The Akashic Alchemist Wisdom School via the books website. For ease, here is the book's website: www. carleenalarayoga.com/the-akashic-alchemist | password: Alchemist999

ALCHEMICAL TOOLS FOR INNER SPRING

Some of the most potent alchemical tools for Inner Spring involve using your voice and your thoughts, as this Season is Divinely Masculine, having to do with the mind and spoken word. Thus, practices that support the harmonization of the throat chakra can also be supportive during this Season. Strong and vigorous exercise can be helpful to some to cultivate motivation, as movement practices can help burn off anxiety or clouds of confusion. Lastly, you can find resources for Anger Release Exercises on the book's site.

- Meditation
- Setting intentions
- Tracking pings
- Keeping an organized planner
- Anger release exercises
- Journaling/Affirmations
- Singing
- Mantra/chanting meditation
- Planning a garden
- Vigorous / strong yoga
- Any form of movement or exercise

CYCLE THREE:
INNER SUMMER

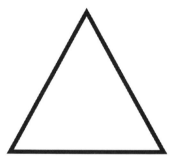

IT'S YOUR TURN
TO TAKE UP SPACE

Long ago
there were fragments of you
that believed
they needed
to be left
behind.

Cast aside
from the fast pace of the world,
you splintered
in many directions.

Too big.

Too loud.

Too much.

Too fast.

The world has many opinions.

But isn't this 'too muchness'
the very same energy
that birthed this entire realm?

We were born to be too much.

We came from exploding stars, after all.

INNER SUMMER AT A GLANCE

PRIMARY ELEMENT
Fire

PRIMARY EMOTION
Joy

PRIMARY CHAKRA
Solar Plexus (Manipura)

GIFTS OF THE SEASON
Passion, Pleasure, Play
Desire
Awareness
Authenticity
Intuition
Community
Connection
Optimism
Sexuality, sensuality, intimacy
Inspiration
Spontaneity
Empowerment
Confidence
Responsibility & reliability
Feeling capable
Harmonious self-discipline

DIVINE FEMININE SHADOW OF JOY
Low energy
Easily manipulated
No follow through
Low self-esteem
Shame
Sadness
Victim mentality, blaming
Attraction to stimulants
Vulnerable to Abuse
Enmeshment
Spiritless

DIVINE MASCULINE SHADOW OF JOY
Overly aggressive
Need to be right
Manipulative
Attraction to sedatives
Violence
Stubbornness
Competitive
Arrogant
Excessive control
Hyperactive

INNER SUMMER AT A GLANCE

DIVINE MASCULINE SHADOW OF JOY
Compulsive
Mania
Abusive
Authoritarian

PHYSICAL ISSUES
Eating disorders
Digestive disorders
Ulcers
Diabetes, hypoglycemia
Muscle spasms, muscle disorders
Chronic fatigue
Hypertension
Disorders of stomach, pancreas, heart, small intestines
Speech issues

TRAUMA
Shaming
Inherited Shame from caregiver
Authoritarianism
Enmeshment
Parentification
Physical abuse
Living in a dangerous environment
Fear of punishment

ALCHEMY PRACTICES
Metta (loving kindness) meditation
Self-love practices
Empowerment/confidence practices
Heart coherence meditation
Vigorous exercise (pilates, running, HIIT)
Martial arts/self-defense
Affirmations
Sun Bathing
Self-Pleasure

AFFIRMATIONS
I am. I am. I am.
I am capable.
I am the spark that creates positive change in my life.
I am learning how to love myself.
I burn through fear with the fire that lives within me.

A LEAP OF FAITH

"You do not have to be good. You do not have to walk on your knees for a hundred miles through the desert repenting. You only have to let the soft animal of your body love what it loves."
- Mary Oliver, "*Wild Geese*"

Three weeks into acclimating in Thailand, and shortly after my concussion symptoms faded and injuries healed, I decided to go on my first weekend trip. Wanting a little vacation before I hunkered down with my studies, I landed on an ancient city on the edge of the jungle nestled high up in the north of the country. After a simple hour and fifteen minute flight, I found myself in a beautiful backpackers town called Chiang Mai. Considered the Buddhist capital of Southeast Asia, Chiang Mai's landscape was adorned with majestic temples, some built as early as the 14th century. The city was rich with culture and abundant sensory stimulation.

Arriving too early for my hostel check-in, I searched around the open-aired community lobby to find something to do to pass the time. Making my way to a bountiful showcase of tourist flyers, I eyed up what activities I could do. Mostly because I was trying to pass the time, I was curious to find out what adventures were accessible.

Gathering a handful of pamphlets and returning to my table, I passed a group of four English lads around my age with their own scraps of paper scattered all over their table. They were laughing at one another's jabs and had this overall air of playfulness. In a moment of blossoming confidence, I decided to invite myself over to their party.

Boldly, I approached this table of four handsome lads, asking if I could join their afternoon plans. At that time in my life I had *never* invited myself to hang with strangers. Prior to this weekend trip, I was going through an internal process of struggling to make new friends at school and feeling myself become reclusive. I set the intention to begin putting myself out there and stepping out of my comfort zone on this trip, and thus, I stepped out on a limb and asked to join their party. With open arms and half menacing smiles, they welcomed me to join their group. After an hour of debate they had *just* deciphered what they were to do for the day: bungee jumping!

Now, I consider myself an adventurous type. At four years old my parents couldn't find me for a frightening few moments at the swim club, only to discover that I'd snuck away and gotten a lifeguard's attention, asking if I could jump off the diving board. I was already on the edge about to jump (with the lifeguard in the water ready to spot me) until they'd realized I had snuck away! I had big plans to someday go skydiving, paragliding or to ride street bikes through windy roads in South America. But bungee jumping?! Fuck *that*. That was where I drew the line! I never had any interest in relying my entire life on a stretchy cord tied around my feet. As I sat at the table with these unfamiliar men contemplating my life's choices before I even checked into my room, I began to wonder why I had interjected at all.

Yet as I looked around at this table I saw a group of best friends who couldn't wait to get out and see the world together. Could I really just go back to my room and be okay with continuing on in my life? Nah – my adventurous spirit won the battle in my mind and two hours later, instead of checking into my room just yet, I was riding in the back of a semi-covered pickup truck through the foothills of rural Thailand, making our way to the bungee stop. During that car ride I laughed until my sides hurt at the novelty of it all. I realized I could choose to follow my desires and that the world wanted to receive me. I was allowed to follow my gut and it felt okay to take some risks. I felt on cloud nine; that is – until it was actually my turn to climb up to cloud nine and jump off of it!

It wasn't until I stood on the edge of the tiny platform, high above the jungle, that parts of me began to question what I was doing. How did I end up here, about to bungee jump – something I swore I'd never do – when I just arrived on vacation only hours ago? Anxiously I began to regret my decision and asked for the staff to kindly take me back down to earth, please. My autonomic nervous system kicked on and was ready to flee and I needed some serious moral support. Hearing my name being chanted from below, I apprehensively looked down to see my four new friends, rooting for me in their cheery accents. They believed in my capability to do this. Turning to my guide on the platform, he smiled at me sweetly and said, "*Take a deep breath and look out at the jungle. Imagine when you jump that all of Mother Earth will catch you. She will.*" His words conjured courage within me to take that step up the edge, lock my eyes on the horizon of the trees and jump with

my arms out, trusting that Mother Earth would catch me
–

Plummeting through the air while simultaneously
feeling like I was flying switched on an unparalleled level
of life force. As I screamed from the depths of my soul, I
felt euphoric. The experience was liberating and terrifying
and magnificent, all at the same time. Such can be the
essence of life. There came a glorifying moment when my
bungee cord grew taut, catching me and springing me up
and down – this moment was a much-needed reminder
that I was tethered to something after all. Once on the
ground I was greeted with high fives and people that
picked me up and swirled me in celebration. The hugs that
make you know you're with your people.

I ended up spending my entire vacation with these four
Englishmen, white water rafting, enjoying family style Thai
meals near waterfalls and visiting the vibrant markets. We
marveled at the majestic nature of elephants and they
supported me when I protested for their animal rights.
They kept me company as I got a tattoo on the nape of my
neck while we watched *The Silence Of The Lambs*. We
danced until 5am in the clubs and bought silly bracelets
that said dirty things on them – the definitions of which
you could only find written on Urban Dictionary.

Looking back on that first day in the hostel I can see
how the trajectory of that weekend could have gone many
different directions, yet I followed that intuitive ping of
desire – the impulse that came before my self doubt. My
desire to make the most of my weekend there led me to
experience moments of pure aliveness. I found people who
were willing to encourage me to jump, reminding me that I
was capable and that I would be safe – people who
ultimately celebrated me in my joyous accomplishment of
doing the damn thing. I realized during that weekend trip,

just days before my classes began, that I wanted more times like these. Belonging. Community. Play. Adventure. If it was possible for me to find a squad in the mountains of northern Thailand, it was possible for me to find them anywhere.

WHAT IS INNER SUMMER?

"One must never let the fire go out in one's soul, but keep it burning."
- Vincent Van Gogh

Once you've compassionately navigated your way through the Obsidian Temple of Shadow work during Inner Winter, to then have set loving-kind intentions in Inner Spring, you arrive in Inner Summer. This fiery phase is all about expansion, nudging you to increase your self confidence and go for what it is that you *really* want. Buried beneath the societal conditioning and programming of your life experiences lies your authentic desires: the pulsating force that swells within, leading you to experiencing more pleasure. Inner Summer isn't a time to play small or give in to disempowering beliefs. This is the Season where we put down our bashfulness and trade it for Jonathan Van Ness-esque swag and authenticity. It is when we come into our own.

Ruled by the Heart, Inner Summer encourages us to prioritize what feels joyful and fulfilling for the soul. In order to discern this, we need embodied awareness and presence – which we cultivated in Inner Winter –as the Heart often communicates in feelings and subtle sensations rather than words. For example, while watching *The Volcano: Rescue From Whakaari*, a Netflix documentary which highlights the courageous civilian rescue of tourists trapped at an erupting volcano in New Zealand, almost all of the survivors interviewed reported a similar feeling of uneasiness that day. On the boat out to the active island, many passengers became physically ill while others felt indescribable waves of anxiety run through their bodies upon arriving on land. Our Heart is always communicating to us, even if we don't consciously interpret the downloads. This part of us is our intuitive network that not only warns us, but inspires us to seek out more of what will help us feel Joy. Inner Summer is a perfect time to learn the language of your Heart.

In Five Element Theory, Summer correlates to the Fire Element which holds the qualities of passion, expansion, pleasure and authentic uniqueness. This Element is connected to the internal Fire you feel when you're lit up about a creative project, social commitment or desire. Fire also teaches us about boundaries, which can swing to either end of the polarity: being contained and even constrained, or billowing out like a raging wildfire.

When in harmony, our Inner Summer fulfills our basic human emotional needs to be seen, felt and witnessed by others. We are creators, creatrixes and creative beings who have incarnated to manifest realities based in heart-centered desires. There is a part of us that finds pleasure through celebrating with other beings who are doing the same. Honoring and revering one another's unique talents and respecting that each of us have a place at the table attunes us to the frequency of Joy. Inner Summer is when we are working in conscious collaboration with people who

WHAT IS INNER SUMMER?

allow us to feel belonging – which is feeling safe to let your freak flag fly. Like our ancient ancestors that spent ample time gathering around the tribal fire, we are social beings who require one another to not only survive, but to thrive.

Inner Summer and the Fire Element connect to the emotion of Joy. Joy is different from happiness, as Joy bubbles up from within the wellspring of the soul whereas happiness is entirely dependent on something external that is triggering it. This emotion of Inner Summer can ironically be present when simultaneously feeling other Emotions like grief or sadness, as Joy from a spiritual perspective is less about pleasure and more about contentment. According to *The Book of Joy* by Nelson Mandela and The Dalai Lama, Joy is "*a way of approaching the world"* and includes making meaning of experiences and experiencing connection.[1]

Inner Summer threads into the third *chakra*, or third yogic energy center, which is called *manipura* in Sanskrit. *Manipura* has many translations, one of which is "lustrous jeweled city." This internal realm full of priceless gemstones and brightness – that was inside of you all along – is only illuminated to you after you apply heat and pressure to the body, mind and soul, burning away the conditioned layers. That heat, called *tapas*, is the catalyst that creates change. For some, we find our inner gems through trials by fire – the archetypal no mud, no lotus hero's journey that is the cornerstone of Buddhism. For others, we find that lustrous bejeweled city through small acts of mindfulness, prayer and devotion, which add up over time, slowly shifting the balance of perspective to cultivate Joy in the long game.

In short and in summary, Inner Summer is a time to alchemizc self doubt into confidence and authenticity. Ruled by the Fire Element, it is a time to expand outward into your community to cultivate belonging, so you have your soul family around you, supporting your highest evolvement. The ruling Emotion during this time is Joy, which is a soft contentment with what is.

SEASON	EMOTION	ELEMENT	GIFTS	INNER ALCHEMY
Inner Summer	Joy	Fire	Belonging, Authenticity, Play	Transmute judgment into Joy

GIFTS OF INNER SUMMER

When you're struggling to taste the sweet nectar of Joy in life, consider engaging with the Inner Alchemy practices of Inner Summer. We will explore more about some of these practices in the chapter *Alchemy of Inner Summer.*

- Passion
- Pleasure
- Play
- Desire
- Awareness
- Authenticity
- Intuition
- Community
- Connection
- Optimism
- Sexuality
- Spontaneity
- Empowerment
- Confidence
- Responsibility & Reliability
- Feeling Capable
- Loving Kind Self Discipline
- Intimacy
- Inspiration
- Sensuality

THE MAGICK OF FIRE

"Step into the fire of self-discovery. This fire will not burn you, it will only burn what you are not."
- Mooji

Just under 14 billion years ago, or so the theory goes, our entire observable universe was condensed into the size of a peach, unimaginably dense, roiling with temperatures of over a septillion degrees. Happening faster than a literal blink of an eye, this fruit-sized nugget of matter exploded and expanded by 10^{78}, through a process called inflation[1]. This was the most violent and transformational time in our universe, known as the Big Bang.[2]

Within twenty minutes the explosion cooled enough to birth the first of the simple elements – hydrogen, helium and lithium. Over millions of years these elements coalesced to become stars and later, groupings of stars called galaxies. The infant universe went from being something you could hold in the palm of your hand to an unfathomably massive realm of possibility that continues to expand more and more with every single second that passes.

Due to gravitational pressures, ancient stars underwent nuclear fusion within their cores. Nuclear fusion is when two atomic nuclei of a light weight combine to form a single heavier nuclei while releasing significant amounts of energy. Overtime, this fusion runs out of material to fuse together. After running out of nuclear fuel, which on average takes anywhere from 50 million to 20 billion years, stars eventually die. Depending on the mass of the star, upon their death some will implode in colossal events like supernovas or kilonovas. These dazzling occurrences provide the final components that life within the Universe needs for its development: they birth the heaviest elements that are necessary for life such as zinc, iodine, and selenium, for example. These heavier elements, which are required for the healthy functioning of sentient life, could not be created by the process of nuclear fusion alone as they require an even more aggressive process that we see unfolding as these supernovae. The most turbulent occurrences in our universe catapulted the fundamental building blocks for life across the universe, in the form of the elements.

The periodic table of elements neatly showcases the chemicals that allow for life to occur. The nitrogen and oxygen that we breathe to survive. The calcium and phosphorus that support the function of our bones. The zinc that fosters cellular regeneration and regulation of a healthy immune system. These chemicals that are alive within us today came directly from the heart of stars. In the words of Carl Sagan, an iconic astronomer and astrophysicist, "*we are made of star stuff.*"

Over billions of years our oldest ancestors – the elements – have been hard at work. Shapeshifting between the three states of matter, all of the elements have had experience as gas, liquid and solid. Experimenting to find their most sustainable state, they've transformed themselves over eons, dying only to be recycled and reborn into future generations again and again. Nothing in our universe has stayed the same. Continuously refueled in the Universe's great forge, the world dies and is reborn again and again with each passing moment.

If it weren't for the Fire, the sacred spark that creates change, we would not be here today. Source Consciousness said yes to a desire of birthing life in this realm and that yes shapeshifted a peach pit into an unfathomably massive divine playground. Not only did Fire birth our Universe, our home galaxy, and our Great Mother Earth – this Element greatly shifted the course of human history, expediting our evolution as a species with its discovery.

Fire has been a sacred symbol in human cultures for millennia, representing the spark of life, the light of knowledge, and the transformative power of creation and destruction. In ancient tribal communities, fire played a central role in the life of the community, providing warmth, light, and the means for cooking food. But fire was more than just a practical tool. It was also a symbol of community and connection, bringing people together around a shared source of warmth and light. In many cultures, Fire was seen as a sacred entity, with its own spirit or deity who was honored through rituals and offerings. The magickal quality of Fire is that of Transformation.

TRANSFORMATION

The archetypal symbolism of Fire represents the energy that creates change. As the great poet Rumi has said, *"In each moment the fire rages, it will burn away a hundred veils. And*

carry you a thousand steps toward your goal." We can offer what
no longer serves us over to the fire to be transmuted into
something new. I work with the symbolism and power of
Fire often, especially when I host ceremonies like my new
and full moon circles. I love to facilitate a burn ceremony
where we journal on three things we are releasing to the
Fire, such as outdated beliefs or habits. Then we write
down three things we want to call into our lives. Using Fire
as the conduit for change, we burn both lists after doing a
relaxing meditation and ritual. We not only burn what we
are releasing, but we also burn what we are wanting to
manifest. This symbolizes releasing attachments and
trusting the Universe to provide the transformation we are
looking for.

My experience of learning how to work with Fire has
come from my own self study of my ancestral lineage of
the Taino, who are the Indigenous people of the
Caribbean; through my journey as a Moon Dancer,
attending ceremony every October with the Mexica people
of México; and from sitting with mother ayahuasca with
the Shipibo people of Peru. I've learned that the living
energy of Fire has been used since ancient times to purify
the body and spirit, helping people to release dense or
stagnant energy and to reconnect with the innocent self.

On an embodied level, I've experienced powerful
changes within me, sparked from Fire in *Temazcales*.
Temazcales are shamanic sweat lodge rituals that are
practiced by ancient civilizations throughout Central &
North America, such as within the Toltecs, Aztecs and
Mayan lineages. Here, the sweat lodge represents the
cosmic womb of all creation, where we return back to the
Divine Feminine archetypal Mother Goddess. Hot stones,
called *piedras,* which are also referred to as *abuelitas*, or
grandmothers, are brought in to heat the cosmic womb

using plant fronds dipped in water to create steam. The stones are considered some of our oldest ancestors that have watched millennia pass by, holding much wisdom. This is why they're referred to as the *abuelitas*. When heated, the Fire activates the grandmother's wisdom within the stones to be transmuted into smoke, which carries divine messages, and this smoke is absorbed through your soul while in the *Temazcal*.

The *temazcal* itself represents the Water Element and the cosmic womb; *las abuelitas* or the stones, represent the Earth Element; the Fire which heats up *las abuelitas* of course symbolizes the Fire Element; and through combining all these other elements together, smoke – representing the Wind/Wood Element – rises and purifies the mind body and spirit, initiating change and offering divine downloads.

I have had many profound experiences during such rituals, including vulnerable releases and shedding lifetimes of energetic baggage. Working with Fire can be intense and stretches my edges of my comfort zone quite a bit. The intensity of the heat creates a unique alchemy that combines all of the Elements together for transformation. Like the serpent shedding its skin, working with Fire is like stripping away an outdated identity, standing naked and vulnerable to yourself and the world. This nakedness – the supple and soft exposure of being seen as you authentically are – is the only way you can feel the cosmic heartbeat and align to your soul's blueprint path. Like a newborn whose skin is so delicate it can feel the pulse of her mother, you, too, can experience a potent connection that only comes from baring it all. Fire is a powerful Element because it strips away the masks and layers, empowering you to shine your brightest.

WHAT IF JOY BECAME YOUR TEACHER?

"Discovering more joy does not save us from the inevitability of hardship and heartbreak. In fact, we may cry more easily, but we will laugh more easily too. Perhaps we are just more alive. Yet as we discover more joy, we can face suffering in a way that ennobles rather than embitters. We have hardship without becoming hard. We have heartbreaks without being broken."
- Archbishop Desmond Tutu

I believe it is your birthright to experience a life of Joy. Following what brings you Joy is the catalyst to reclaim your most magnetic self. This intuitive pilgrimage of pursuing the breadcrumbs of Joy requires discernment, as this emotion can easily move out of harmony if it's misunderstood. Joy is a state of inner calm that lives within your Heart. When you allow yourself to be exactly where you are, unattached to seeking constant pleasure or avoiding pain, you immerse yourself in the present moment. In the present moment, Joy can arise as a sweet feeling of fulfillment and contentment. Even in turmoil one can experience Joy.

Spiritual Joy can be understood as a humble, sustainable and content feeling that continues to self-generate from the Heart. This Emotion can be found even on the darkest of days, even when we're not necessarily happy. Joy arises when we are consciously creating meaning from life experiences and this chosen perspective is what can either provide us with a sense of acceptance and contentment or, alternatively, suffering.

This Emotion is misunderstood to be ecstasy and pleasure, brought on by some sort of stimulus. When we seek it outside, or seek a continuous need for feeling comfortable, it actually pushes Joy further away. The alchemy of Inner Summer includes transmuting judgment into Joy so that you can experience the sweet contentment of life more often.

TRAUMA THAT SHAPES JOY

Below is a brief list of various traumas that could impact the development of your Fire Element, which in turn affects the harmonious expression of Joy.

- Shaming from caretaker
- Authoritarianism
- Parental domination
- Enmeshment
- Parentification
- Physical abuse
- Living in a dangerous environment
- Fear of punishment
- Inherited Shame from caregiver

PHYSICAL, EMOTIONAL + MENTAL MANIFESTATIONS

Below is a brief list of possible physical, emotional and mental issues that can manifest from a dysregulated Fire Element.

- Eating Disorders
- Digestive Disorders
- Ulcers
- Diabetes, hypoglycemia
- Muscle spasms, muscle disorders
- Chronic fatigue
- Hypertension
- Disorders of stomach, pancreas, heart, small intestines
- Speech issues

Note: *This list is inspired by Traditional East Asian Medicine, Ayurveda and Tantrik Yoga Philosophy.*

PRACTICES THAT ALCHEMIZE JOY

- Metta (loving kindness) meditation
- Self love practices
- Empowerment/confidence practices
- Heart coherence meditation
- Vigorous exercise (pilates, running, HIIT)
- Martial arts/self defense
- Affirmations
- Sun Bathing
- Self Pleasure

ALCHEMY OF INNER SUMMER

"I used to think I was the strangest person in the world but then I thought there are so many people in the world, there must be someone just like me who feels bizarre and flawed in the same ways I do. I would imagine her, and imagine that she must be out there thinking of me, too. Well, I hope that if you are out there and read this and know that, yes, it's true I'm here, and I'm just as strange as you."
- Frida Kahlo

The long days and shorter nights of summer provide us with an opportunity to connect more with nature, receiving the abundance of life force energy straight from our solar sun. In many spiritual traditions, the sun is seen as a representation of the Divine Masculine father archetype. It is a source of light, warmth, and life-giving energy that inspires us to feel capable, empowered and aligned. This season also subconsciously channels us with abundant social energy to connect with one another, as many ancient cultures hosted large and abundant festivals during this time of year.

In ancient times our oldest ancestors would honor the arrival of summer – the season of abundant expansion – with rituals to honor planetary and cosmic alignments like the Summer Solstice. Lighting massive bonfires, hosting extravagant feasts and giving offerings to the growing crops were common practices seen around the world.

During summer we enjoy the longest days of the year, offering our subconscious psyches a subtle boost of vital energy that inspires us to gather together. Gathering in conscious community is one of the most healing things we can do, as it gives us a practice ground for rewiring outdated beliefs and provides us with a wellspring of inspiration. Seeking conscious community is another way of saying to spend time with groups of people who are actively working on growth, evolution and self awareness, to support themselves, their communities and humanity. Right now we are seeing a mass awakening for the need of having conscious communities to support our internal biological need of connection and supporting the rising of consciousness on this planet.

This passionate season is ruled by the Fire Element. Fire has been used for eons as a symbol of desire, creative inspiration, social gathering and transformational alchemy. It is a powerful force that can purify and transform what is old and stagnant into something new and vibrant. Many Indigenous cultures, and some of your eldest ancestors, view Fire as a living Spirit with profound power that we can work with to evolve. We can use the energy of Fire to inspire our own creativity and passion, to release what no longer serves us, and to embrace new beginnings.

When you engage with Inner Summer's Emotional Teacher of Joy and explore this Season's alchemical practices, you are able to receive the gifts of this season, namely: belonging, inspiration and authenticity.

BELONGING

Joy is certainly a self-generated Emotion, but it does not mean we can only find it alone. Our search for Joy cannot be undertaken in isolation, as we are social creatures who do best when teaching, learning and co-regulating with one another. We need others to help us along the way, to provide support, inspiration, and a sense of safety. Belonging, then, is not just a desire or a luxury, but a fundamental need for spiritual growth and well-being. Belonging is a feeling of support and safety that arises when there is a sense of inclusion, acceptance, and shared identity. It's the feeling we get when we're with our people.

When we feel a sense of belonging, we are able to relax into a state of being that is more open, receptive, and loving. We are able to transmute our Fears and insecurities more easily by having support and safety. When we feel disconnected and alone we can become trapped in a state of Fear and anxiety, unable to see beyond our own limitations and struggles because we don't have any trusted people to reflect back to us the magick of who we really are. Prolonged loneliness has serious health implications and disrupts our nervous system, becoming either defensive and overly protective, or closed off and apathetic.[1] In highly individualistic countries like the United States, we've been conditioned to self-isolate, prioritizing hyper-independence which has long term and detrimental effects on our health. We were never meant to heal alone.

As we explored, the ruling Emotion of Inner Summer is Joy, which is a self-generated experience of contentment with the present moment. Because we are social beings, our biology is hardwired to more readily produce contented and Joyful states when we're relaxed, spending time with trusted people. The experience of spending time with conscious community can create an experience of co-regulation.

According to Polyvagal theory, co-regulation is when there is reciprocal sending and receiving of signals of safety between two people or more.[2] For optimal health and well-being, we need to have a balance of self-regulation (which we cultivate in Inner Winter via resourcing inner safety) *and* co-regulation (which we explore by seeking belonging in Inner Summer). Spending time with a trusted loved one can create these reciprocal signals of safety, reminding your nervous system that you are welcomed to be your authentic self.

Belonging is a feeling of support and safety that arises when there is a sense of inclusion, acceptance, and shared identity. When you're doing alchemical work during Inner Summer, you are not only finding belonging with others, but also with yourself. This Season, how can you give every part of you a seat at the table? Your Highest Self, Inner Child, Inner Teen, Shadow, etc. We live in a mirror Universe, where the things you believe about yourself will be reflected back to you as your perception of reality. If you do not allow parts of yourself to belong, it will be difficult to believe you belong in community. In many ways, this Season is about deepening your sense of self love through giving yourself permission to feel whatever it is you're feeling, moment to moment and day by day. This is a reminder that Joy, the ruling Emotion of Summer, is a sweet contentedness with what is. Your present self, or your grounded self that is not filtered by your conditioned history, can find Joy even as your Inner Teen within you is feeling sacred rage. Your present moment loving awareness can experience Joy even when your Shadow is triggered by an old wound. Within you there can be a dialogue between these parts of self, where your loving alchemist awareness can say, "*I know you're feeling xyd right now, and that's okay. You belong here and your feelings are valid.*"

I do not believe in the statement, "*you cannot love another until you can love yourself.*" I believe that other people can actually *remind* us to love ourselves and show us how. When you feel safe in someone else's presence, and they are not judging you, it sends subconscious cues to you to also not judge yourself. We are keen at modeling behavior, and sometimes it is the reflection of compassion and unconditional love from another that initiates it within you. When you're on a quest for belonging, be sure to pay attention to how you feel in the presence of others.

ALCHEMICAL PRACTICE FOR BELONGING: MANIFEST YOUR SOUL FAMILY

You can manifest anything, including friendships! Attracting your soul family to you will create a strong foundation for you to express yourself, network and collaborate on your dreams. It also initiates co-regulation, allowing you to rewire outdated patterns of regulating safety alone, moving into co-creating it in community. Here is how I manifested some of the most significant relationships in my life where I finally feel that I belong:

- In your journal make a list of all the qualities you desire in your relationships. Attentive listening, interest in similar hobbies/topics, or personality traits you're attracted to like compassion and giving back to humanity may be things on your list. You can even include things you don't want, like gossiping, for example. Ask your nervous system: *what traits, behaviors and qualities in others create feelings of safety within me? What creates feelings of unsafety?* Keep adding and editing this list. This list makes it easier for you to spot certain qualities you enjoy in others, and will make those moments of connection that much more special, as your soul rejoices from belonging!

- As much as you can, embody the friend you want to be. Like attracts like. When you embody the friend you want to attract, you will magnetize those types of people to you. Be diligent to stalk your own Shadow here, as you may find that you're embodying old, outdated patterns that are not on your friendship manifestation list. Hold compassion for yourself when you slip into older patterns, while consciously choosing to show up within the new timeline you're creating.

- Step outside of your comfort zone and attend events that would have the types of people you want to meet there. Ecstatic dances, concerts, new/full moon circles, kirtan and yoga classes are places where I've met some of my most adored and aligned friendships.

- When you meet someone you're drawn to, nurture that relationship through reciprocity and gratitude. Learn and ask questions on who they are and how they wish to be loved and supported, and practice embodied, active listening. Trust that the people who are meant for you will reciprocate. You will not be for everyone and that is okay. You *will* find your people.

AUTHENTICITY

Engaging in hobbies and experiences that satisfy your soul brings out a luminescence that is radiant and attracts more people to you that have similar interests, as like attracts like. When you give yourself permission to follow what brings you Joy, you become magnetic. When you feel afraid of judgment, this can stifle your authentic self expression and block your magnetism, as you're sending out confusing signals to the Universe. At the root of fear of judgment, though, is actually a projection of inner judgements that you hold towards yourself. You will never feel threatened by judgment from others if you aren't judging yourself.

One of the greatest gifts of doing alchemical work, namely Shadow Work, is authenticity. Shadow Work illuminates your unconscious belief systems that may be ruling your perception. As the infamous psychoanalyst Carl Jung says, "*until you make the unconscious conscious it will direct your life and you will call it fate.*" In my Embodied Business Mentorship, I see many women struggling with unconscious judgments that arise when they want to leave their jobs or start a new career in spirituality or wellness, for example. *What will my family think of me when I start sharing about my past and my childhood? Will the people from high school judge me if I start sharing about sacred sexuality or astrology? What will people at my current job think about me if I start sharing about my interests I have never talked about?* These are all ways we can see that deep down, there is some part of you that is judging yourself. Through doing Shadow Work, journaling and hypnotherapy, you can alchemize these parts of self that are judging through compassionate understanding.

When I left my stable job to run my soul led-business, I navigated a lot of judgment which I saw reflected back in my fears of others judging me. I did hypnotherapy and learned that the younger, twenty-year-old atheist who believed spirituality was stupid was sitting as the CEO in my business' mind. She was a people-pleaser, terrified of being judged by others and adapted her personality to fit in everywhere she went. It was exhausting! My work was to hear her, honor her and her fears during that age, while simultaneously promoting my present self to CEO.

My twenty-year-old self still has a place at the table, but she is doing her Inner Alchemical work to transmute her judgments as my present self remains the boss. Through this Inner Alchemy, I am releasing the need to please everyone, accepting that I may not be liked by everyone, and affirming that I am still safe to authentically self express myself. It all started from continuously reflecting, each time I felt judged, on what this was revealing on how I was really feeling in relationship to myself.

ALCHEMICAL PRACTICE FOR AUTHENTICITY: I BELONG

It's easy to continue at a pace that moves quicker than the heart and soul desires to. This alchemical tool will support you in slowing down and receiving your heart's authentic feelings and desires. This is a powerful tool. I recommend doing this every day for one week to see what you notice.

- Create a space for meditation. Consider playing

soft music and either sitting up comfortably or lying down.
- Bring one hand to your heart and take 3 deep breaths as you turn your attention here. Feel the spaciousness that already exists here. Breathe in through your nose and out through your mouth.
- Ask yourself these questions/affirmations:
- *What does my heart yearn for?*
- *What is it that I want to create today?*
- *I love you, I'm listening...*
- Journal or reflect on what your heart had to say to both of these invitations. Allow your Heart's feelings to have a place at the table, giving them permission, reminding them that their feelings are valid and they belong.

PLAY

A huge component of Inner Alchemy is acknowledging the different parts of self that coexist with your present moment awareness, and one part to acknowledge is your Inner Teen. For many of us there lies an unprocessed grief that came from subtly moving from childhood to adolescence, when the conditioned worries of the world began to creep in. There came a time in life when we learned Santa wasn't real, we were looked at weird for speaking to our imaginary friends or when our favorite games were no longer picked up because our friends didn't think it was cool anymore. A part of us was left behind, no longer able to express their playful nature because life started to teach us to be serious.

Play is considered a social need for children as it teaches emotional intelligence, promotes collaboration and reduces stress. Emerging research on the effects of play in adulthood highlights that the positive psychological effects don't only affect children, but adults, too![3] While editing this book, I navigated some frustrating moments of self doubt, confusion and overwhelm. I had approaching deadlines and an internal sense of pressure as my inner perfectionist was making an appearance. At the brink of burnout I decided to heed my own advice and double my devotion, spending some more time meditating with my guides and praying for guidance. After asking for help my guides asked me, *"When was the last time you had fun? When was the last time you made time for play?"* Upon hearing this question I began to sob as I realized that my inner child and inner teen had felt abandoned in this creation process!

From this intuitive guidance, I set an unwavering intention: each week I will schedule time for play! Whether it be a game night with friends, dancing to music I loved as a teen, or roller skating, I return back to the activities I loved as a kid to replenish myself on a soul level. Play has the power to create new neural networks of Joy.

ALCHEMICAL PRACTICE FOR PLAY: INNER TEEN EMBODIMENT

- Make a list of some of the things that inspired Joy within you as a child or teen. Did you dream of being a mermaid or astronaut? Did you love to swim or play kickball? What were some of your favorite past times? Make a list of your favorite hobbies, games, books, movies and memories.
- Schedule time for play! Send out that group

text or schedule a solo date between your Inner
Teen and your adult self.

SUMMARY: ALCHEMICAL TOOLS FOR INNER SUMMER

Inner Summer Alchemy has to do with welcoming all parts
of you home, promoting feelings of belonging. This Season
is Divinely Masculine and has an "outward" quality, just as
Fire likes to expand outwards in all directions. This
symbolizes our social needs of being seen, heard and felt
by our community. Anything that promotes self love or
expanding your confidence helps you alchemize self doubt
or judgment into Joy and authenticity. Practices that
support the harmonization of the solar plexus chakra can
also be supportive during this Season.

ALCHEMICAL TOOLS FOR INNER SUMMER

Inner Summer Alchemy has to do with welcoming all parts
of you home, promoting feelings of belonging. This Season
is Divinely Masculine and has an "outward" quality, just as
Fire likes to expand outwards in all directions. This
symbolizes our social needs of being seen, heard and felt
by our community. Anything that promotes self-love or
expanding your confidence helps you alchemize self-doubt
or judgment into Joy and authenticity. Practices that
support the harmonization of the solar plexus chakra can
also be supportive during this Season.

- Metta (loving kindness) meditation
- Self love practices
- Empowerment/confidence practices
- Heart coherence meditation

- Vigorous exercise (pilates, running, HIIT to burn off excess "Fire")
- Self Pleasure
- Martial arts/self defense
- Affirmations
- Sun Bathing

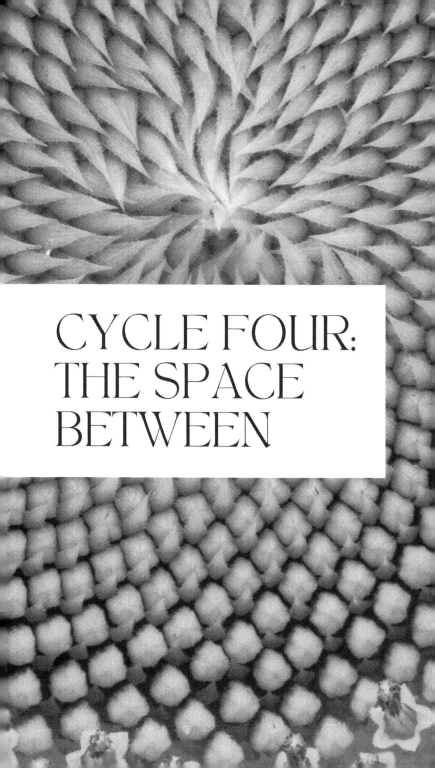

CYCLE FOUR: THE SPACE BETWEEN

MEMORIES OF THE PAST

[Original Nahuatl Translation]
Ica ohtken eyazqui
Amitla ni tenyo titlio
Tlacuitlalpan tlalipan
Quiniqui xuixino yolotzin
Axemotopalli xihuala
Nemilicoeponiz tlalipan
Tinezcayo totiuh xochime
Tinezcayo totiuh cuicame

[Spanish Translation]
Memorias del pasado
que dejaré cuando me vaya

No es acaso que en vano venimos
sembremos al menos flores
dejemos al menos cantos
no es acaso que a eso venimos

{English Translation]
Memories of the past
that I leave when I go

It is not in vain that we come

We plant at least flowers
and leave at least songs

It is not by chance that we come

Memories of the Past by Abuela Malinalli

THE SPACE BETWEEN
AT A GLANCE

PRIMARY ELEMENT
Earth

PRIMARY EMOTION
Empathy

RELATED CHAKRA
Root Chakra (Muladhara)

GIFTS OF THIS SEASON
Compassion
Caring
Devotion
Giving
Receiving
Grounding
Reliability
Reciprocity
Gratitude
Generosity
Fertility
Comfort
Being of service
Understanding
Abundance
Prosperity
Fulfillment
Satisfaction
Integrity

DIVINE FEMININE SHADOW OF EMPATHY
Demanding
Seeking attention
Neglectful
Disassociation
Poor boundaries

DIVINE MASCULINE SHADOW OF EMPATHY
Codependency
Rejecting support
Hyper-independence
Compulsive giving
Rigid boundaries

PHYSICAL ISSUES
Eating disorders
Chronic fatigue, sluggish
Disorders of bowels, anus, large intestine, spleen
Disorders of solid parts (bone, teeth)
Frequent illness

TRAUMA
Birth Trauma
Abandonment
Physical neglect

THE SPACE BETWEEN
AT A GLANCE

TRAUMA

Poor physical bonding with mother
Malnourishment
Feeding issues during infancy/early
childhood
Issues during pregnancy
Major illness or surgery
Physical abuse or violence
Inherited ancestral traumas

ALCHEMY PRACTICES

Earthing (bioelectric grounding)
Physical touch
Being of service to humanity
Hypnotherapy for early childhood
Birth trauma healing
Nurturing the mother wound
Ancestral healing
Nervous system regulation
Body image work/mirror work
Gratitude journaling
Law of attraction/Manifestation
Affirmations
Somatic release exercises
Trauma and Tension Release
Exercises (TRE®)
Massage
Yoga

AFFIRMATIONS

It is safe for me to be here.
I love my body and trust its
wisdom.
I attract all that I desire.
I am abundant.
My needs are always met.
The earth always provides for me.

I REMEMBER

"Thank you mother earth, for holding me on your breast. You always love me no matter how old I get."
- Ruby Modesto, A Cahuilla Elder

Drifting between lucid dreams, altered states and moments of conscious awareness, my physical body grew each day in the warmth of my mother's womb. From peanut to person my cells worked hard to clone themselves, following an ancient code of evolution. As her traveling companion for nine months, and she mine, my mother's heartbeat was the very first sound I heard. The cosmic pulse of life that whispered to me without words, energetically saying, *'don't worry, I am here. I will always be here.'*

Threaded together through a cord of unconditional giving, I was tethered to my mother as her life became the sustenance that gave me mine. Endlessly providing for my needs around the clock, I was hidden beneath the surface of her baby bump that continuously grew, regardless of whether or not she felt ready for me to arrive.

My mother was the very first person who told me a

little bit more about the world I was going to enter into through the vibration of her life print during those nine months. As miraculous as it is to welcome new life into the world, my mother's discovery that she was pregnant with me was the metaphorical catalyst that initiated the changing of her life as she knew it. Wiggling around in my mother's womb, my little kicks were reminders to her that I was coming as I listened to more than just her heartbeat.

Three months into our pregnancy my dad was shot just a few inches below his heart and required life saving surgery, cutting open his entire abdomen to remove the bullet fragments. When my mom received that phone call, I was there. Although he spent weeks courageously doing so, my father graciously made a full recovery. By divine intervention, the day my father was shot, he happened to jump in his place from being startled at seeing a gun pointed at him. This last minute reflex meant the bullet grazed the bottom of his heart, saving his life. At three months in gestation, my ears had just finished developing. I sat and listened, as the witness to life on the outside, through the reverberation of sound that moved through my mother. I heard the abundance of my mother's cries throughout those nine months, many of which kept her up at night. Sitting in her belly I wished I could hug her and tell her someday it would all be okay.

As our pregnancy waxed on, my mother went through another initiation of trust. At twenty-four weeks our amniotic sac ruptured, which means her water broke at five and a half months. In most cases, when this happens it means the baby will need to be delivered prematurely, oftentimes happening within days of the rupture. At the time, twenty-four weeks was the cutoff of gestational viability – meaning doctors did not medically think an infant could survive and live a healthy life if born at twenty-four weeks or less. My mom was admitted to the hospital where they brought in grief counselors, specialists and an entire team who seemed to be bracing her for the worst.

My mother listened as they suggested many solutions to a growing problem, poking and prodding her in the name of survival. During a time of emotional turbulence, my mom was sitting up in her hospital bed beside a nurse that was comforting her, holding her hand as specialists entered the room. Some of the best doctors in the region advised her, with urgency, to undergo an invasive bone marrow test to learn why the amniotic sac broke. The nurse that had been holding my mom's hand squeezed tightly in a non-verbal way, discreetly sharing her opinions that were different from the doctor's. My mom chose to trust that nurse in all of her divine feminine compassion and nurturance and opted out of the procedures.

One evening while we were hospitalized, my maternal grandfather lay praying. He was not a spiritual type, but the risk that his daughter and future granddaughter faced was enough to bring him to his version of God. As he lay in bed praying he – for the first time – saw an apparition of what he believed to be the Holy Ghost, appearing to him as flames. He could only describe this moment as a washing over of peace; he intuitively felt that it was a sign that all would be okay. This mystical experience he had coincided with the same time my mother got the news that my amniotic sac was miraculously healing over – a very rare occurrence. Although I'd still be a high risk pregnancy, I wouldn't be arriving at 24 weeks.

Four months later, late into an October night under the full moon, my mother and I went into labor. They placed monitors on my head and discerned that I was in distress.

My birth was quickly changed from a vaginal birth to a c-section.

Before I knew it I felt myself being pulled from my first and only home I ever knew. I remembered how cold it was when I was pulled out of the tiny incision they made into my mother's womb, a suction released full of blood and life. I greeted a world with fluorescent lighting and harsh, metallic infrastructure.

How uncomfortable it was to not be able to move my arms and legs at will! How frustrating that my desire to go to my mother's breast only came out as unconscious cries! I felt the fierce chill on my naked body as they whisked me away for testing, knowing through the thread of our psychic umbilical cord that my mother was as cold as I was. My request to be in her arms, communicated through my screams, was denied by medical staff. In those precious first moments I didn't get to touch her and feel her skin, her heartbeat against mine.

My earth side origin story is a marvelously complicated one. Full of worries, doubts, trust and faith – my arrival was embedded with conflicting emotions. And on October 25, 1991 at 7:03 am I was welcomed into this world with unconditional love as my parents held to their faith in our soul agreement.

Before my arrival in my mother's womb there was a cosmic yes between my parents and me. When I was a star child, I chose them so they could teach me a little bit more about life on Earth. But I didn't just say yes to Ramona and Luis becoming my caretakers. I said yes to our entire lineage and all of the familial genetics, nervous system life prints, subconscious patterns, soul contracts, and karma that they individually and collectively held in their ethereal DNA. I entered this world holding the keys to my ancestors and their prayers for our lineage.

WHAT IS THE SPACE BETWEEN?

"All we have to decide is what to do with the time that is given us."
- J.R.R. Tolkein

Depending on where you live on Mother Gaia, there comes a time once a year where ripe fruit hangs low on the branches and harvest is most abundant. Equal days and nights of steady temperatures soften the need to do, allowing more space to meander and be. Here in the Northeastern corner of the United States, we experience this transient period during late August to early September. Somewhat a season in its own right, it may be known as *Late Summer.*

In Five Element Theory, Late Summer represents a window of cosmic suspension, where the archetypal energy of the Earth is not waxing (rising and expanding) or waning (falling and diminishing). It is the zero sum point of neutrality. Our physical and emotional bodies do this same cosmic dance between contraction and expansion all year. This season of Late Summer, which I call The Space Between, is a time of energetic stability that gives us a sweet reprieve before we spiral into the underworld of Inner Autumn.

Ruled by the Earth Element, this phase and its corresponding Element is neither yin nor yang. The Space Between is a transitional phase of engaging harmoniously with the world around you, celebrating your abundant harvest. When the intensity of Inner Winter calms and you become open to intuitive insights and healing. After the trials and tribulations of Inner Spring quiet and you receive that clarity you have been seeking. When the Heart becomes inspired again to follow its desires in Inner Summer. The Space Between is the transitional point during any season where you are called to relish in the abundance of life's bounty.

You may have heard Pierre Teilhard de Chardin's infamous quote, "*we are spiritual beings having a human experience.*" One of the initiations of The Space Between is to transcend mundane worries that we have no control over and place our attention on the bigger picture. How do you want to be of service to yourself, your community, humanity, and our Great Mother: planet Earth. There comes a time where you feel a sweet nudge to ask yourself, *what is it that I am really doing here? What is my purpose?*

The Space Between is a unique phase because it not only represents *Late Summer*, but the space between all the Seasons. You may have noticed that there is a subtle energy that creates a bridge between summer and fall, autumn and winter, the darkness into spring and spring into summer. It is the nurturing energy that sweetly transitions us through the seasons. This harmonic energy that gently carries us from one season to another is also ruled by the Earth Element. It is stabilizing, gentle and balanced.

The Space Between can also represent the Season when you are navigating a transitional period of life, seeking a sense of grounding and stability. It is when you're alchemizing worry and overwhelm into gratitude. It arrives as a quest to tap into an abundance mindset rather than lack and zero in on a purposeful life. This phase teaches you how to call upon your inner mother to create inner stability, self-soothe and nurture yourself through the moments when you feel out of balance.

In short and in summary, The Space Between is a time to cultivate the gifts of Abundance and Ancestral Healing.

SEASON	EMOTION	ELEMENT	GIFTS	INNER ALCHEMY
The Space Between	Empathy	Earth	Abundance, Ancestral Healing	Transmute Mother Wound into Inner Mother

GIFTS OF THE SPACE BETWEEN

When you're contemplating how much you're giving versus how much you're receiving, consider engaging with the Inner Alchemy practices of The Space Between. We will explore more about some of these practices in the chapter *Alchemy of The Space Between.*

- Abundance
- Ancestral Healing
- Inner Mother
- Compassion
- Purpose
- Caring
- Devotion
- Giving
- Receiving
- Grounding
- Reliability
- Reciprocity
- Gratitude
- Generosity
- Fertility
- Comfort & Safety
- Being Of Service
- Understanding
- Prosperity & Wealth
- Fulfillment
- Satisfaction
- Integrity

THE MAGICK OF EARTH

"Let us be the ancestors our descendants thank."
- Winona LaDuke

Rotating at 1,000 miles per hour and barreling through the solar system, Earth simultaneously travels 67,000 miles per hour around the sun. This centrifugal force – along with expanding nuclear heat in Earth's core – are the balancing acts that prevents our celestial home from collapsing in on itself. Our planet comes equipped with an inherent way to resist the crush of gravity, keeping all of life in harmony. Within our macrocosm of the Universe, as dark energy – the opposing force to dark matter – rapidly expands our Universe, the continuous coalescing of gas and particles inversely come together through the opposite force of gravity.

We see this balancing act not only in the planets of this Universe, but in the very tissues of our bodies. Through bio-hydraulic expansion of our myofascial tissue and electromagnetic heat within our cells, our bodies manage to oppose the same force that dropped Newton's apple. We come equipped with technology that allows us to stay upright without getting crushed by gravity ourselves. Within every corner of the observable universe we see one thing in common: there is an underlying structure of harmony woven into all things. All animals have this intelligence. All plants have this technology. Our ancient elders and ancestors knew this.

According to the ancient philosophy of Five Element Theory, the Earth Element corresponds to its own mini season called 'Late Summer.' Unique to the Earth Element, this archetypal energy doesn't just show up once a year, but also between every season, as Earth is the bridge between all phases. Source Consciousness designed this realm from a wildly intelligent perspective. Graciously, we do not catapult between seasons but instead have a window of time where we are in a meeting place of both. Earth energy arises two weeks before the change of seasons and sweetly carries us from Winter to Spring, Spring to Summer, Summer to Autumn and Autumn to Winter.

In our psycho-emotional world, the Earth Element is the archetypal energy that fosters reciprocal relationships, creating a bridge between us and other people. Relationships that are balanced in giving and receiving foster deep bonds rooted in trust, mutual cooperation and reciprocity. The Emotional Teacher of Earth and The Space Between is Empathy.

Material in form, the Earth Element also includes all things 3D: your physical body, your health and wellness and your relationship to this planet. This Element also represents the patterning around managing daily tasks that provide stability like paying bills, managing time and your relationship to work, for example.

In many ways, the way you nourish and nurture yourself as an adult showcases the maturity of your Inner

Mother. Your Inner Mother is an archetypal energy inside of you that takes care of you with unwavering understanding and love, while also holding you accountable and responsible for life. Part of the alchemical work this Season is about learning how to mother yourself as the most supportive, compassionate and dependable caretaker you could imagine, as only you know exactly what you need.

There are a few phases of early childhood that have molded your Earth element – and your Inner Mother – the most: womb development (gestation), birth, the bonding phase and the separation phase. Through Inner Alchemy practices you can "mature" your inner mother, transmuting any pain that you may have learned or inherited as an infant and young child, initiating the process of ancestral healing.

WOMB DEVELOPMENT (-9 TO 0 MONTHS)

Development of your inner Earth Element began before you were born. Chemical and hormonal signals were transmitted to you via the placenta throughout the entire journey of your mom's pregnancy with you. This means you felt every emotion she did, with the same intensity. You received your first experiences of the world around you while in the womb and these energetic imprints were stored in your subconscious as feeling-based memories.

Your time spent in the womb is also when epigenetic markers were laid down on your genes. Epigenetic markers are little tags that tell genes to turn 'on' or 'off' during your lifetime. These markers tell your genetic sequencing – or your DNA coding – whether or not to express particular traits throughout your lifetime.

Epigenetic markers laid down during pregnancy have

been correlated to behaviors and neural patterning that can manifest in the infant's future adulthood, such as how well they manage stress throughout their lifetime or the potential to develop obesity or eating disorders. More recently, scientists are hypothesizing that epigenetics could be partially responsible for ADHD, Autism and other neurodivergent patterns. Epigenetic tags also place markers down that can affect the manifestation of alcoholism or risk of other health issues like cancer or heart disease. Essentially, the environmental, behavioral and emotional stimulus that was swirling around you during your time in the womb could have laid down genetic markers for future patterns to emerge.

Anything that your mother navigated while pregnant that created an emotional imprint on her, subsequently impacted the development of your Earth Element. Hesitation about keeping a pregnancy or navigating depression or anxiety before, during or after birth could have impacted your inner child's perception of your world before you even arrived. Suffering from anxiety during pregnancy, experiencing conflict in relationships, or managing stress from work or life circumstances are some examples of how your mom's life during pregnancy could have shaped your Earth Element's expression.

Other Womb Development Experiences That May Shape Your Earth Element: *mom's financial, emotional, physical, or mental well-being during your pregnancy, drug use, significant stress or trauma, difficulty eating or nourishing herself, illness in mom or fetus*

BIRTH (0 MONTHS)

One thing that is seldom spoken about in modern medicine is the importance of birth on our psyches. Birth is the first emotional imprint we have of the physical world and for many of us, it was traumatic.

Trauma means anything that feels too much too fast for the nervous system. Going from a warm water world to a harshly bright and astringent environment after being squeezed out by mom's painful contractions can certainly alter a baby's first perception of the world. First impressions are everything.

The resurgence of midwifery, doulas and holistic coaching for pregnant women feels like we're returning to our ancient ways of welcoming a baby into the world with ease. These practices prioritize the well-being of mom not only during, but after pregnancy, too. In doing so, this translates into the wellness of the growing soul within her. There is a need for culturally and socially responsible training and understanding within these fields to promote safe, equitable and vibrant birthing practices.

Other Birth Experiences That May Shape Your Earth Element: *needing emergency intervention during birth (such as a c-section or needing forceps, etc.), inability to have skin to skin contact directly after birth, difficult labor, birth injuries, hospital birth*

THE BONDING PHASE (0 TO 18 MONTHS)

Postpartum, also known as the fourth trimester, is a significant window of time that molds one's Earth energies, in addition to the first two years or so of life. The primary themes that affect this Element's development are how well you received nourishment, attachment and support as a baby. This is directly connected to your relationship to your mother during this time.

The manifestation of Empathy was most heavily influenced by the holistic wellness of your mother during your development in her belly and the nourishment/support you received during your first few months on Earth. Mom's wellness includes her physical health/dietary choices/exposure to chemicals/pesticides, overall stress levels, psycho-emotional states, additional responsibilities to care for other siblings and all other environmental influences like work and interpersonal relationships. Nourishment and support includes adequate nutrition, attention, skin to skin contact, holding and support. The subconscious relationship you have with your birth mother is the largest contributing factor to the development of your Earth.

Some of us may have experienced clear neglect, abandonment or rejection of needs as infants. Others may have had the most well-intending mother who gave much of herself to support healthy growth. Regardless of the narrative, through the eyes of an infant's nervous system, no mother can meet every need of a child exactly when the need arises. An example of this could be when a baby goes down for a nap in their crib and mom decides to take her first shower in days. The baby wakes and cries to express its needs of perhaps hunger, thirst or a desire to be held. Unavoidably, mom cannot move faster than she already is to rinse the shampoo out of her hair, get dried off and go hold them to feed. From the eyes of the child who has no concept of time but biological impulses of basic needs and feelings, the duration it took mom to arrive could energetically feel like abandonment or neglect.

Receiving adequate nurturing and support during your

infancy could have been disrupted by many run of the mill circumstances:

- If mom was hesitant about her energetic, financial or physical capacity to have a baby during pregnancy.
- Prenatal and postpartum depression or anxiety.
- Difficulties breastfeeding or limited access to nutrient dense formula.
- Being isolated or separated from mom directly after birth. The birth of a younger sibling within the first eighteen months.
- Mom having a medical condition, illness or an inability to provide enough attention or holding.

There are many circumstances in which our mother's capacity to nurture and support us as infants molded the development of our Earth Element, affecting our programmed perception of feeling held, supported and important.

Witnessing my sister, friends and family members go through the initiation of birth and motherhood has been life altering for me. I began growing a deeper and fervent respect for mothers all over the world. Old enough to see this phase through a different lens, I observed that the women I know received the least amount of support during the fourth trimester, perhaps when they needed it most.

Our ancient ancestors used to live in tribal communities that would share the responsibilities of caring for a newborn child, including tending to the well-being of the mother. For many global and domestic reasons, we have lost this small-size community-based support and now rely on government assistance to sustain maternity leave, which is unfortunately a systemic privilege.

The International Labor Organization (ILO) which established international recommendations for maternal health guidelines for women advises that maternity leave globally should be no less than fourteen weeks, although it is suggested to be at least eighteen. UNICEF (The United Nations Children's Fund) – an international organization that intends to provide healthcare and aid to children all over the world – recommends that this time be at least twenty-four weeks.[1] If maternity leave is even accessible, it averages four to ten weeks paid time off in the United States – a staggering statistic that falls unequivocally short to human rights organizations and international standards.

Proper nourishment, energetic feelings of stability/safety provided by our environment and proper attachment/attention from mom are necessary for optimal development of our Earth Element. There are many reasons why even the best mothers can be disrupted in their care of their child, such as needing to return to work or occurrences like injury, illness or getting pregnant with a second child. What's important to note here is that most of us have had some disruption to our Earth Element, regardless of our mother's parenting style or well-being during our infancy. This is most likely due to systemic and cultural practices that often have mothers feeling isolated or unsupported themselves during child rearing.

Other Bonding Phase Experiences That May Shape Your Earth Element: *postpartum depression, feeding issues, anxiety or depression in mom or primary caregivers, living in an unsafe environment or with too much stressful stimulus, neglect, abandonment, caregivers' inability to provide skin to skin contact and holding, physical illness in mom or you as a baby, arrival of a* *younger sibling during this time, primary caregivers (especially mom) needing to return to work during this time.*

SEPARATION PHASE (18 - 24 MONTHS):

At some point you crossed a threshold between needing your mother and desiring to explore more of the world around you. Depending on how your mother processed and nurtured this initiation also molded your Earth. When this happens too soon, on a nervous system level you may have felt abandoned, which is a feeling that happens independently of thought. When this happens too late, it becomes more challenging to create an individual identity of your own personal needs.

This phase of life is what creates ripples that manifest as adults in relation to your ability to give and receive. This can later have implications with money, time and responsibility. This phase also shapes the Emotion of Empathy, which is the Emotional Teacher that correlates to Earth. We'll explore this in depth in the next chapter.

WHAT IF EMPATHY BECAME YOUR TEACHER?

"We are more alike my friends than we are unalike."
- Maya Angelou

The ruling Emotion of The Space Between is Empathy and it is the emotional bridge between sentient beings. It is the act of energetically taking yourself into the realm of someone else's experience, feeling what you imagine they are feeling as they navigate a tender time. This Emotion – of being able to shapeshift into another's emotional landscape – is what creates the unconscious experience of feeling supported and nourished by your relationships, strengthening your compassion muscle. In many ways it is your connection-making superpower.

In order to feel Empathy, one takes themself into the emotional context of what another person is going through in order to courageously feel that energetic texture *with* them. Exchanging Empathy within intimate relationships nurtures a bond rooted in trust, support and understanding. It is a basic emotional need, as we have evolved to be complex social beings who require reciprocal relationships in order to feel stability, safety and support. In the most harmonious expression, when you're empathizing with someone, you are holding an embodied presence yet you do not need to say or do anything to comfort the other person. Empathy isn't advice giving or giving pity. It manifests as pure presence, active listening and embodied energetic support. To simply *be* there with another while they are going through a tender time can initiate a powerful alchemical process, forging meaningful bonds between you and that person.

If we haven't done alchemical practices yet, our ability – or inability – to provide and receive Empathy is an unconscious process, regulated by the autonomic nervous system which was shaped in early childhood. The development of your capacity to give and receive Empathy mostly evolved psychologically between gestation in the womb through to twenty-four months of age, as we explored in the chapter *The Magick Of Earth*. Your relationship to giving and receiving Empathy as an adult is correlated to the interchanges of experiences between you and your mother during your pregnancy, infancy and early childhood.

Here is an example of this. Let's say during early childhood your parents got pregnant again and another little one joined your family. Perhaps your parents were overwhelmed working a job, taking care of the household and parenting more than one child. It is common for older children and middle children to develop unconscious wounds of abandonment, neglect or rejection once the little sibling arrives, as they no longer are the primary focus of attention.

Let's imagine that you are holding an unconscious hurt from feeling abandoned or neglected by your caretakers, and are seeking creative ways to get this basic social need met. One way you could try is to seek, or even demand, attention, which is a manifestation of an unbalanced Earth Element: the child doesn't receive the basic need of attention and so they seek it out unconsciously. Another way you could receive this attention is through helping out around the house. This behavior could be positively reinforced with affirmations and loving attention from your parents, presumably from their gratitude for you helping them when they're overwhelmed. Overtime, this reinforcement of being supportive can create people-pleasing tendencies later in life, or an imbalance of prioritizing other people's needs over your own, because it is unconsciously linked to receiving love, attention and praise.

In short, your ability to be in a reciprocal relationship with yourself and with other people is molded from your time in childhood. The interplay between you, your caretakers and your siblings created an unconscious patterning of behavior that molded how safe you feel asking for your needs and how much capacity you have to offer support to others' needs.

As a loving reminder, you come equipped with an uncanny ability to transform outdated, unconscious behavioral and neurological patterns through doing embodied alchemical practice. Basically, nothing is set in stone, including the patterns created in early childhood. *You* are the alchemist of Empathy.

TRAUMAS THAT SHAPE EMPATHY

Below is a brief list of various traumas that could impact the development of your Earth Element, which in turn affects the harmonious expression of Empathy.

- Birth Trauma
- Abandonment, rejection
- Physical neglect
- Poor physical or emotional bonding with mother
- Malnourishment
- Feeding issues during infancy/early childhood
- Issues during pregnancy
- Mental illness of mom
- Major illness or surgery
- Physical abuse or violence
- Inherited Ancestral Traumas

PHYSICAL, EMOTIONAL + MENTAL MANIFESTATIONS

Below is a brief list of possible physical, emotional and mental issues that can manifest from a dysregulated Earth Element.

- Eating disorders
- Chronic fatigue, sluggish
- Disorders of bowels, anus, large intestine, spleen
- Disorders of solid parts (bone, teeth)
- Frequent illness, hypochondria
- Narcissism
- Codependent disorder
- Attachment anxiety

Note: *This list is inspired by Traditional East Asian Medicine, Ayurveda and Tantrik Yoga Philosophy.*

PRACTICES THAT ALCHEMIZE EMPATHY

- Earthing (bioelectric grounding)
- Hypnotherapy for early childhood
- Maturing inner mother
- Mirror/body image work
- Birth trauma healing
- Being of service through your dharma
- Physical touch, massage
- Ancestral healing
- Gratitude journal
- Embodiment
- Any form of physical movement

ALCHEMY OF THE SPACE BETWEEN

"You have come to earth to entertain and to be entertained."
- Paramahansa Yogananda

Late Summer is a time when nature hangs in the balance. The abundant harvest from half the year's work is ready to be enjoyed and is a natural space to feel gratitude for such bounty. This appreciation for the Earth and her abundant gifts creates a sweet reciprocal relationship between us and the world around us, repairing and repatterning any fears of lack. This time symbolizes a harmonious balance between light and dark, as the days gradually shorten and darkness begins to increase. It reminds us of the importance of finding balance in our own lives.

Just as the sun and the moon coexist, representing opposing yet complementary forces, late summer teaches us to integrate various aspects of ourselves — such as work and leisure or activity and rest — to experience harmony.

Late Summer is associated with the Earth Element. The Earth Element represents stability, nourishment, and grounding. During this time, we are reminded to nurture ourselves and others in a reciprocal way, to care for our physical bodies, and to cultivate a strong foundation of our Inner Mother. This symbolism emphasizes the importance of self-care, self-love, and tending to our own well-being like the most unconditionally loving caretaker.

When you engage with The Space Between's Emotional Teacher of Empathy and explore this Season's alchemical practices, you are able to receive the gifts of this season, namely: Abundance and Ancestral Healing.

ABUNDANCE

Abundance is a way of being, which means you live a life focused on the plethora of bounty that is around you at all times, rather than what is missing. You can either live a life in a lack mindset, or in an abundance mindset. Abundance mindset believes that there is enough for everyone versus competing for minimal resources. In my online Manifestation Courses, I teach students how their early childhood shapes their relationship to abundance. *What did your caretakers make money mean and how did they use money?* Many of us have Shadows around this. When it comes time to manifest prosperity, we may carry unconscious beliefs about the interchange of money into the picture, or subconsciously focus on the 'not having' of it, which only perpetuates a lack mindset more.

Abundance mindset also includes your relationship to receiving. Bringing in more wealth is a practice of receiving, meaning you must be open, willing and receptive to the new energy flowing in. In my work with clients around money and abundance we usually do hypnotherapy to not only repattern old, outdated beliefs about the meaning behind money, but also our ability to give and receive in general. Then, we implement gratitude practices and practices that prepare to be in the receiving mode.

ALCHEMICAL PRACTICE FOR ABUNDANCE: GET INTO THE RECEIVING MODE

One of the foundational teachings of Abraham-Hicks, a prominent inspirational speaker on the topic of manifestation, law of attraction and abundance mindset, is learning how to get into the receiving mode. Here are some ways to get into the receiving mode, as per these teachings:

- **Create time to meditate.** Meditation is one of the best ways to raise your vibration and come into energetic alignment with what you want. If you're feeling unworthy, depressed, resentful or drained, it is hard to become a magnet for what you want, because you're like two opposite ends of a magnet, pushing abundance away. When you meditate, you raise your vibration through feeling any repressed feelings and organizing the clutter of your mind, making it easier for abundance – which is a high vibrational state – to find you. Consider this energetic and mental maintenance.
- **Start a Rampage of Appreciation.** Abraham describes a rampage as one subtle thought that moves into the next, gaining momentum as you go. When you're feeling low energy or in lack, choose one thought that is slightly closer to abundance than where you are currently at. Keep doing this, shifting your focus slowly, until you gather momentum. It's a

practice of cultivating a rampage of gratitude that tells the Universe, *I am already abundant.* When you acknowledge and celebrate what you already have, you are in the receiving mode.

- **Believe that everything is working out for you.** This is a powerful belief to put in place. Over time it will strengthen your trust muscle with the Universe and open you up to believe that you are worthy of abundance. We live in a mirror Universe that reflects back to you what you authentically believe, and so if you believe everything is working out for you, it does.

Note: I *have met many clients who learn about the law of attraction who develop a fear of "low vibrational feelings," afraid that they won't ever be able to manifest what they want. Manifestation is a complex energetic topic and requires inner alchemy practices to transmute your relationship to your Emotions, not getting rid of entire Emotions. The alchemy of abundance does not include bypassing how you feel in order to feel "high vibrational." If you want to learn more on this subject, I invite you to explore the manifestation programs that I offer. (*Head here for more www.carleenalarayoga.com/ the-akashic-alchemist | password: Alchemist999)

ANCESTRAL HEALING

Like the Universe, all humans began as a tiny metaphorical peach. Ripe with the infinite potential to become anything, we were forged in our mother's core. We all began as two cells: one egg plus one sperm, which reproduced rapidly just like the elements that formed our early universe. It is estimated that the average adult *homo sapien* has up to thirty to forty trillion cells in their body. Their ancestors all traced back to those two cells. Our bodies carry an entire universe of life.

Traveling within your cellular and molecular biology are the imprints of your ancestors' lived experiences. Like whisper down the lane, ancestral trauma is passed down quietly between generations. Ancestral trauma can manifest differently between each descendant in your lineage, making it harder to spot. This means you may be holding on to shame, guilt or pain that was never yours to carry.

Your grandparents most likely navigated hardships like the great depression, immigration, war, inaccessibility to education or wellness services, scarcity mindset, discrimination, oppression, PTSD, unemployment, substance abuse, domestic violence, or physical hazards at work – the list goes on and on.

Biologically female fetuses develop all of their eggs within their wombs during development. This means that the egg that became you was inside the womb of your mother, when she was in the womb of your grandmother. This means that a part of your molecular biology was in the womb of your grandmother, vibrationally feeling everything she did.

The descendants of your grandparent's generation – that of your parents – held these memories on a cellular and molecular level while they themselves developed in the womb. The manifestation of this in adulthood could look like your parents repressing emotions, continuing substance abuse or violence, having a dysregulated nervous system, overly focusing on external stimuli like work or codependent relationships, and often having untreated mental illnesses.

Transforming itself once more, this cellular pain makes its way into your lived experience. Perhaps it is in the form of anxiety or depression, resistance to vulnerability, mistrust, self sabotage, imposter syndrome, people pleasing, seeking attention or struggling to understand who you are. Your body remembers what they tried to forget. Scientists are now postulating that our molecular biology holds the energetic imprints from multiple generations before us. This is why ancestral healing is important.

Ancestral healing is the practice of addressing and healing patterns of trauma, pain, or unresolved emotions that have been passed down through our family line. These patterns can include physical or emotional ailments, relationship struggles, financial challenges, or any other issues that seem to persist despite our best efforts to heal or improve them.

In many spiritual traditions, it is believed that our ancestors continue to influence our lives long after they have passed away. These influences can be both positive and negative, and can manifest in a range of ways. For example, we may find ourselves repeating the same relationship patterns as our parents or grandparents, struggling with similar health issues, or facing financial challenges that seem to have no logical explanation. Ancestral healing involves recognizing and addressing these patterns, as well as the emotional and energetic imprints that have been passed down through the generations. It is a process of connecting with our ancestors, acknowledging and honoring their experiences and wisdom, while also releasing any negative patterns or emotions that no longer serve us.

Through ancestral healing, we can break the cycle of suffering and create a more positive future for ourselves and our descendants. By acknowledging and releasing the negative patterns that have been passed down through our family line, we can create space for new, positive patterns to emerge. We can connect with our ancestors in a way that allows us to feel more grounded, empowered, and connected to our roots.

Many Indigenous, Earth-based cultures practice forms of ancestral connection, opening up psychic and intuitive channels to receive wisdom, guidance, healing and affirmation from loved ones who have passed. Ancient cultures from all over the world such as the druids and ovates of Celtic people from Ireland knew the importance of managing our holistic wellbeing to consciously stop the ancestral cycle of pain. Modern science is now catching up to this wisdom through the study of the epigenome. When channeling ancestral wisdom, one does not have to look far as the information that is sought lives within one's own molecules and cells.

ALCHEMICAL PRACTICE FOR ANCESTRAL HEALING: LEGACY WORK

When I was facilitating 200 Hour Yoga Teacher Trainings, we taught an exercise called Legacy Work. Legacy work is when you make lists of legacy traits you inherited, some of which are behavioral, cultural, genetic or philosophical. You then make two lists: one is a list of all the things you want to KEEP, setting intentions to keep these traits alive for future generations. The second list is compiling all of the things you want to RELEASE, setting the intention to energetically shed unhelpful patterns to liberate yourself and future generations. To see this full exercise, head to the book's website and step into the alchemical portal.

CYCLE FIVE:
INNER AUTUMN

THE GUEST HOUSE

"This being human is a guest house.
Every morning a new arrival.
A joy, a depression, a meanness, some momentary awareness comes as
an unexpected visitor.
Welcome and entertain them all!
Even if they're a crowd of sorrows,
who violently sweep your house
empty of its furniture,
still, treat every guest honorably.
He may be clearing you out
for some new delight.
The dark thought, the shame, the malice, meet them at the door
laughing,
and invite them in.
Be grateful for whoever comes,
because each has been sent as a guide from beyond."
- Rumi

INNER AUTUMN AT A GLANCE

PRIMARY ELEMENT
Metal

PRIMARY EMOTION
Grief

RELATED CHAKRA
Heart (*Anahata*)

GIFTS OF THE SEASON
Comfortability with Impermanence
Reverence
self-worth
Value
Adapting to change
In tune with instinctual nature,
primal self
Perfection of the moment
Acknowledgement
Spaciousness
Appreciation
Allowing
Purity
Refinement
Sacredness
Balance of spirit + body
Non-attachment
Acceptance of self, others, and life
circumstances
Peaceful

DIVINE FEMININE SHADOW OF GRIEF
Inability to hold on
Difficulty making meaningful
relationships
Fear of intimate relationships
Withdrawal
Isolation, loneliness
Critical of oneself, inner critic
Sadness
Low self-worth
Rejecting compliments
Inability to acknowledge one's
preciousness

DIVINE MASCULINE SHADOW OF GRIEF
Inability to let go
Jealousy
Ruthless seeking of external
gratification
Hoarding
Dogmatic beliefs
Obsession with achievements
Perfectionism
Critical or overly righteous
Aversion to experiencing loss

INNER AUTUMN AT A GLANCE

PHYSICAL ISSUES

Lung or Heart issues
Addiction to smoking
Issues of Large Intestine
Constipation
Tension between shoulder blades
Asthma
Allergies
Pain in chest
Difficulty breathing, shallow breath
Bronchitis
Pneumonia
Immune System Issues
Skin issues

TRAUMA

Rejection
Abandonment
Shaming
Betrayal
Cold environment without love
Abuse from Father Figure
Unacknowledged grief
Divorce
Loss of a loved one
Sexual or physical abuse

ALCHEMY PRACTICES

Present moment awareness
practices
Breathwork Practices (*pranayama*)

ALCHEMY PRACTICES

Building an altar
Inner child healing, Nurturing
Father Wound
Mindfulness
self-worth Practices
Somatic Release Exercises
Processing Grief
Embodiment of Primal Self
Journaling
Doubling devotional practice
Connecting with a higher power
Connecting with spirit guides
Connecting with highest self
Gratitude practices
Meditation
Forgiveness (*Ho'oponopono*)
Yin Yoga
Hypotherapy
Mantra meditation

AFFIRMATIONS

All I have is this moment and this
moment is precious.
I am worthy.
There is infinite and unconditional
love all around me.

"I'm sorry. Please forgive me. Thank you. I love you."
- Hawaiian Ho'oponopono Prayer

I felt the nourishing breeze floating in from the Arabian Ocean as I nestled into the backpack town of Varkala, India. Staying at a quaint hostel – it's patio bursting with tropical flowers, I was enjoying my yogurt parfait with fresh pineapple and cantaloupe as birds flitted around the flowers searching for their own breakfast.

While enjoying some of the world's most delicious fruits I happened to overhear a guest at the hostel on the phone talking about how some American girl was going to host a Thanksgiving dinner for the groups of backpackers staying at the local hostels in town. After spending over a year and a half traveling abroad, I had become quite natural at both eavesdropping and inviting myself into other's plans. After he hung up the phone I curiously asked if I could join the Thanksgiving Dinner. He welcomed me with open arms.

Somehow that American girl managed to locate two

turkeys that the owners didn't mind selling to slaughter, along with two local boys who knew how to break down the bird. Somehow she found a way to find dried cranberries in such a rural backpacking village, rehydrating them for cranberry sauce. Her ingenuity was on point, getting all the fixings for a full spread which would ultimately feed over twenty people.

Gathered around the table on Thanksgiving night I was surrounded by souls from many different countries and cultures, many of whom had never been to a Thanksgiving Dinner. Those of us from the United States shared about the story we were taught in history class versus the true story. The truth being that one of the first Thanksgivings (as there were many during the English invasion) was to celebrate English soldiers after they massacred the Pequot people. During those first 100 years, colonizer soldiers reduced the Indigenous Native American populations by ninety percent in that area. The romanticized and peacefully portrayed Thanksgiving in American textbooks would actually be what we would call today a genocide.

Our table held moments of silence for those who were unjustly massacred on the land they stewarded for tens of thousands of years before colonizer rule arrived. We offered prayers to the native lands that we were hosting our dinner on. Gratitude was sent to the animals that were humanely broken down for our meal and to those who helped make it possible.

This level of reverence I witnessed in everyone during this meal was the first time I had seen a large community actually speak into the real history of Thanksgiving outside of conversations that happened with my family. It was a potent night of acknowledgement of Indigenous culture, prayers of gratitude and rejoicing in the preciousness of the moment.

After our story telling and setting the history straight, we enjoyed our meal while engaging in conversation, getting to know one another as many of us were traveling solo. While discussing music tastes, the person I had been seated next to mentioned he loved trance. He shared that he was going to see Above and Beyond – a DJ group that's legendary in the genre – in Bangalore in a few days. Excitedly I shared how I'd always wanted to see them and wished him an awesome show. I was surprised when he said he had an extra ticket and would love it if I came along. I did have a loose itinerary of staying in Southern India yet I felt an intuitive ping to ditch the plan and lean into the present moment. The next morning we took a fifteen hour train ride from the southern tip of India to *Bengaluru* (Bangalore) City.

During the show, synchronicities continued to unfold as we met an Italian couple and their local Indian friend dancing next to us. We made our own mini dance circle, celebrating one another's authentic self expressions; I felt like I was with my people and could let my freak flag fly.

After the show ended they invited us to an afterparty in the city proper and had extra VIP tickets they wanted to gift us. Following another ping of feeling safe in my body and open in my heart, we made our way to the next part of our night via *tuk tuk*. Along the way we rode in our open air vehicle, similar to a bedazzled golf cart, buzzing our way deeper into the city.

Our group passed an incredible traditional Indian wedding whose festivities seemed to stretch for miles. I saw countless elephants adorned in gold and dazzling paints, wrapped in garlands of flowers and jewels. Throngs of people were dancing and singing, hearing their enlivened songs grow in their intensity, only to fade as our *tuk tuk* whizzed by.

We pulled up to a modern yet ornate venue where I was impressed to see it was an official, private party hosted by MTV and VH1, boasting some incredible DJs on the lineup. Walking through heavy wooden doors with ornate carvings, my senses were flooded with incredible visuals, pleasant scents of rose and jasmine and the most amazing lighting and sound. I'll never forget going to the bathroom on a heated toilet which appeared to be coated entirely in gold. I had never seen anything as lavish as this place.

We spent many more hours dancing until the lights came on and in the wee hours of the night we got in a cab headed back to one of my new friend's homes. He was an Indian architect who made a name for himself in Bangalore and had designed his home on the edge of a forest near an airstrip where he owned a plane. We arrived at the home not long after and I was offered cozy pajamas, some tea and soft socks as they put on some music. I melted into the comfort of this place, welcomed as if I was in an old friend's home. Immediately my ears perked up as I heard the unmistakable voice of Jerry Garcia singing the infamous song *Ripple* by the Grateful Dead. I began to cry tenderly from home sickness.

Seeing my tears the architect asked me what home was like. How was life in my country? How was my family doing? What was my relationship like with my parents?

I'm typically an over-sharer with strangers and so I shared the tenderness that was plaguing my heart. Perhaps he could sense it on me. Or maybe he was good at bypassing small talk and getting right to the heart-stuff. Whatever it was, I felt comfortable to share and was so happy he asked.

To rewind for a moment, after I graduated from my master's program I traveled all the way to India to study the path of yoga. During my 500-hour yoga teacher training we were committed to being in class six days a week for two months straight, from 5am to 9:30 pm each day. It was one of the most grueling, emotionally explorative and mind-expanding things I have done to this day. The path of yoga is not just the physical practice, or what we call *asana*. The path of yoga is a way of life, a way of being in the world. It is an all-encompassing holistic practice that permeates all layers of who you are.

And so, rightfully so, all that I had been carrying in my twenty-three years of life up until that point came up and out during my yoga teacher training, like a dormant volcano that had reactivated her power. During the months of my YTT was the first time I had really explored the pain of my childhood on a somatic level. Within those two months I worked intimately with my mentors on how to heal those inner child wounds so that I could forgive myself and my family for the pain I perceived as a child. Growing up in a household with addiction, drug abuse, alcoholism, mental illness, and being first generation greatly influenced my childhood. I realized how much resentment, frustration, grief and pain I was carrying within my body from my upbringing. Narratives of feeling neglected, unimportant and insignificant were beliefs I held that I could no longer avoid. They were coming up and out, asking to be nurtured and transformed into gold through the alchemical work of yoga.

Shortly before my yoga training graduation I received a phone call that my dad had been diagnosed with prostate cancer. The terror of this diagnosis triggered a significant, and understandable fear response within him, leading him down a pathway of unhealthy coping mechanisms from his past. When I learned of this news I felt devastated and enraged. *Why now? Everything was going so well. We were all doing so good.*

Traveling in time now to the conversation with the architect…*How is your family doing? What is your relationship to your parents like?* This was why I was happy he asked.

Vulnerably I shared all of the raw, confusing emotions I was moving through. The diagnosis. My dad reverted back to old vices. Both of my parents in need of support. My inner child wounds were reactivated all over again. As I shared through a shaky voice, I remember feeling tremendously ashamed for the resentment that was coloring my story. Embarrassed that he was seeing what I viewed as my selfish emotions. My dad was given a diagnosis that could affect his entire life and future and here I was, irate with both of my parents and grieving for my inner child again.

Attentively listening and curiously wanting more context, my new found friend asked why my dad developed such vices in the first place to cope with his pain, and I began recounting the many complex traumas that my dad endured in his lifetime. I began to run through the tape recorder of my dad's early life in successive order, zooming out from my perspective for a moment. In that void of timeless time, my compassion expanded like my perspective. I realized I had never shared his inner child monologue in successive order.

Listening intently until the end of my synopsis, tears streaming down his face, he began to laugh and cry all at the same time. In a way that pure coincidence cannot explain, he began to recount painful details of his past that eerily mirrored my dad's. They were both survivors of the same complex abuse, abandonment from caregivers and systemic injustice. They both had to hustle hard to get by without many opportunities. I learned he also had a daughter around my age and he was roughly the age of my dad. My friend shared how he had always wondered how his drug history, mental health issues and his internalized and unprocessed pain from his complex trauma in his childhood affected her.

Knowing this moment was one destined by fate, he offered up that we try an exercise. He would pretend that I was his daughter, so he could apologize to her and say the things he wished he had the courage to say. I would pretend that he was my dad and clear all the things I wished I could say but didn't know how to or when to. Staring into his eyes, it felt as though I was looking into the eyes of my dad. With their similar skin complexions and some similar facial features, when I focused my gaze intently enough it appeared as though I was actually talking to my dad.

This exercise initiated us both to get quite vulnerable as we navigated through our hysterical cries, occasional yells and eventual settling of the emotional currents running through our bodies. After some time we naturally dipped into a space of silent completion, simply gazing into one another's eyes for a time. Within Shamanic cultures and practices, it is said that by gazing into the eyes of another you can see their past lives, your past lives, the connection between souls and receive messages from the Universe. During that time of eye gazing, memories of my dad's childhood flashed into my eyes as if I got to see them firsthand. Some beautiful days and some days that I'd do anything to wish he didn't have to experience. A complete sense of understanding for my dad and his choices and the natural compassion that evolves from such an understanding was something that I still carry with me to this day.

That night I learned quite a bit about sustainable forgiveness. Previous to this evening, I had spent much of my yoga teacher training trying to forgive my parents by reframing my mindset and trying to think about the past from a different vantage point. What I learned in that gorgeous house with the massive windows that overlooked the small airport landing strip was that forgiveness wasn't something to be done, but something to be felt. A somatic release and healing across timelines that can only come from letting the raw primal parts be felt, heard and seen. I had to ugly cry. I had to say the things I'd always wanted to say but would never *actually* say out loud to a loved one. I had to release the pent up rage and grief and acknowledge that my inner child had been hurt. I also learned how to zoom out and see how to hold two things at once. That two things could be true. My pain was independent from my parent's pain. I learned that it felt better to believe we all have been doing our best.

This life changing moment with a stranger was the one that began to mend my relationship with my father, and subsequently with mom, initiating a sense of forgiveness that I couldn't have fathomed otherwise. Over the months that followed, I started to notice all the ways I had repeated the patterns I adopted in childhood. I felt neglected and unimportant – a story I unconsciously adapted myself, as no one had told me that. And I kept that story going through my entire life, without knowing it.

The powerful part was, through forgiving them I also forgave all the times I neglected myself.

WHAT IS INNER AUTUMN?

"To err is human, to forgive, divine."
- Alexander Pope

In early autumn the leaves respond intelligently to the shorter days as they receive softer, less intense sunlight. This initiates a process of letting go. The leaves of broad-leaved trees prepare to fall down towards Earth. Inside the leaves, the veins that transport fluids and nutrients in and out of the leaf eventually sever, conserving energy downwards towards the trunk and roots.

Without this decay process, if these broad-leaf trees were to hold onto their leaves, they would become extremely vulnerable to elements. Eventually they would freeze, crystallizing and damaging the opening at the entrance of the leaf. This would fracture growth for future seasons. Their mastery of the art of letting go is what keeps them alive and thriving for the cycles that come.

Due to soil conditions and temperatures of the summer that came before it, every single autumn leaf expression is unique to that autumn and that autumn only. It's as if

Mother Nature takes off her polished mask of uniformity in green, putting on a magnificent display of wild, vibrant and unique color expressions that are never the same year to year. Every autumn is a rarity, never to be seen again.

The Inner Season of Autumn is ruled by an Element called Metal and the direction of energy flows downward during this Season. In a literal sense, metal can be molded into protective devices like shields or weapons while it also includes precious metals that are excavated from the Earth like gold, platinum and crystals. Metal symbolically represents that which is valuable and in turn, psychologically represents the theme of feeling worthy or unworthy as worth is intrinsically linked to value.

Our overall energy wanes during this time as we are called into the preciousness of every moment. This is the seasonal purpose and mission of Inner Autumn: to hold reverence for life in its myriad of expressions. With subconscious cues of death and decay all around us, we are unconsciously asked to explore this one wild and precious life that we have. Inner Autumn is where we practice merging together our primal, animal self with our mystical, limitless self.

There is a part of you that knows you will reincarnate for many more lifetimes, holding the keys to doors that hold all the information you seek while you simultaneously know this is the only life time that you will ever have as *you*. There will never be another personality and alchemical design exactly like the one you are embodying now in this dimension and timeline. When in harmony, Inner Autumn offers acknowledgement to the preciousness of your unique, multifaceted nature, that will never be seen again in all of the cosmos!

The ruling Emotion of Inner Autumn is Grief, which in itself is a precious human emotion. When Grief is flowing in its divine masculine expression, we unconsciously defend against it and find it difficult to let go. Letting go in this context doesn't mean spiritually bypassing how we feel – it is specifically linked to when we have trouble releasing our grip or attachment to something in order to fill a void of unworthiness.

The Divine Feminine expression of Grief is internalized, where we have difficulty holding on. Again, this Season is connected to self worth, and so if we feel unclear on who or what we value, we may have trouble building meaningful relationships that are in alignment with your self worth and beliefs. This disconnection from others can lead to a sadness that filters life experiences, as we are hardwired for human connection.

Another sub category of Grief is Sadness. Inherent in sadness is some sort of loss or disappointment within the present moment. It may stem from a plaguing nostalgia, sorrow from grief, or from suffering due to wishing life could be different than it is. According to Lonny Jarrett, an infamous teacher of East Asian medicine, we can even experience *"Grief directed at the future."*[1] Grief in Inner Autumn represents not only the physical loss of someone or something but also the metaphorical Grief we can navigate throughout our lives.

SEASON	EMOTION	ELEMENT	GIFTS	INNER ALCHEMY
Inner Autumn	Grief	Metal	Forgiveness, Self-Worth, Liberation	Transmute Father Wound into Inner Father

GIFTS OF INNER AUTUMN

- Comfortability with impermanence
- Reverence
- Self worth
- Value
- Adapting to change
- In tune with instinctual nature
- Perfection of the moment
- Acknowledgement
- Sacredness
- Spaciousness
- Appreciation
- Allowing
- Purity
- Refinement
- Balance of spirit + body
- Non-attachment
- Acceptance of self, others, and life circumstances
- Peaceful
- Connection to primal self

THE MAGICK OF METAL

"Three things cannot be long hidden:
the sun, the moon and the truth."
- Buddha

Katya was a magnetic woman who came to see me for a past life regression therapy session. Her intentions were to deepen her connection to the most important people in her life and heal from old wounds in relationships with her family. Our journey began like any ordinary regression. She was swimming in cool water, making her way towards a tropical island that she called home. When I invited her to take a look at the horizon and describe what she saw, she detailed two medium-size pyramids on the larger island to her left and a small pyramid-like structure on the island to her right. She knew they were used for ceremonies that had great significance to their community. These particular pyramids were used to harness the lunar energy from the moon; she called them moon pyramids.

This scene of her swimming melted right into the next as she now sat around a campfire, seated on logs as seats.

She was surrounded by her entire family and many other relatives, their rich caramel skin dressed in matching chocolate brown woven clothing. They were discussing their preparations for a significant moment coming up: the lunar eclipse was almost here and it was quite a big deal. They were going to travel back to their home: the star system of Pleiades.

On the evening of the eclipse their community filtered into the subterranean chamber of the largest pyramid, holding hands as a part of the ritual. They began breathing together in rhythmic harmonies and sounds, to which she recapped that it took a good amount of time and effort to do just right. After some time, her body (in current day) began irregularly breathing for a few moments until she burst into tears. I gave her some time to feel, before asking what she was experiencing.

The teleportation *worked*. She and her family were finally back home, in Pleiades.

Over the second portion of the regression she told me all about this new plane of existence she cosmically traveled to. Every corner of her vista was adorned in bioluminescent purples and pinks – a gorgeous shimmering washed over all that she perceived. She was surrounded by other beings, who were not in physical bodies per se, but more like vibrating energy. She was overwhelmed by the joy she felt returning home because for the first time in a long while, she felt free.

The purpose of her family going to Earth in the first place was because their souls wanted to learn how to be in community together, specifically on Earth. The difference between their home planet in Pleiades and that of Earth is the vibrational speed/frequency. On Earth we vibrate slower (and thus have a wider range of emotional, physical and energetic sensations available to us) whereas in

Pleiades they vibrated much faster (allowing for greater harmonious frequencies like love, compassion, forgiveness and joy), incarnated as pure energy rather than a body. She detailed how it is easy to be in community when your natural state is closer to love than fear, such as on Pleiades. In many ways Earth was like an intensive school for them, able to teach their souls significant lessons that her home star system doesn't have the capacity to teach. It's like enrolling in a university that comes equipped with certain programs/majors. Earth has many to choose from.

The reason why their mission took much longer than expected was because they were committed to learning how to be harmonious with one another and live compassionately. They didn't return until that felt true. Katya shared that during that lifetime she learned what unconditional love for another human being really means. She learned how to lead with love, no matter the circumstances as they certainly encountered more disagreements, challenges and hurdles on Earth than in their home of the Pleiades star system.

At the end of her regression, in the deepest state of trance, she connected the dots. She felt like her whole life began as a journey to mend the wounds of her childhood, feeling neglected and disconnected from her birth family. This regression reminded her of that unconditional love that was accessible to her, along with what it felt like to be free, without the density of her past weighing her down. She wanted to open herself back up to love again.

As a past life regressionist I've encountered some miraculous souls who have incarnated across different star systems, dimensions and timelines. Their stories have expanded my perception of what is possible in this multiverse, and what has been possible on our cosmic home of Earth. It is not uncommon that I regress people to other planets/star systems that are different from Earth, or regress clients to Earth's ancient history in lost civilizations such as Lemuria, Sumeria and Atlantis.

There are two interesting themes that have emerged through the many clients I've regressed. The first is that advanced civilizations have existed on planet Earth long before main-stream history recounts. The second is that these advanced civilizations used ancient technology that worked intricately and in harmony with the Earth and Her astro/quantum physics to create what some would call magick. An important component in most of their stories that allowed for such alchemy was the use of precious metals and specific crystals like quartz – the most abundant crystal in Earth's continental crust.

In one regression, a client named Amir[1] – told me that the Egyptian pyramids we see today are not the whole picture. They once were tipped with metal points made of gold and other elements at the top. The metal from the Earth was an electromagnetically efficient way to harness cosmic energy in two different ways: solar energy from the sun and lunar from the moon. They had separate pyramids to harness these separate frequencies. These metal tips – which have either been destroyed, stolen or lost from the elements of time, were the crucial pieces to create a functioning pyramid as its original design intended. He told me that the pyramids were once used as chambers to raise our electromagnetic frequency which allowed for rapid and spontaneous healing, amplification of prayer/manifestation and bringing entire communities into states of harmonious frequencies.

Melissa was another client who channeled similar information. She recounted how the pyramids were ancient power generators able to heal and upgrade entire civilizations far and wide and some of the ones we see today across the globe are recreations of much more ancient pyramids that came much earlier in Earth's prehistory. She shared how these megalithic structures were also used to conduct electricity, the smaller metal points on top being the crucial semiconductor to collect electrical charges. When used in conjunction with pools of water, underground chambers and either the solar/lunar energy from the Sun or Moon, an entire civilization could harness this abundant cosmic energy.

When I reflect upon the magick of Metal, my mind pings back to these incredible stories of my clients and their cosmic journeys. I've had over a dozen clients recount, in some way shape or form, that the precious metals and crystals of our planet hold potent power to naturally and sustainably: produce electricity and light, allow for levitation of people/objects, create megalithic structures, raise the vibration of living being's bioelectromagnetic fields and allow for time travel. Metal was considered to be a precious conduit for raising consciousness on our planet, giving us access to "magickal" powers.

In relation to Inner Alchemy, the Metal Element is symbolic for that within you which is precious and valuable. Metal represents your ability to become a conduit for change, able to transmute pain into alchemical electricity to manifest new states of being.

PRECIOUSNESS

Just like the unique leaves during autumn, you too are a multifaceted, irreplaceable work of art. As you walk your sacred path as an Akashic Alchemist, you may notice that no one thinks or feels exactly as you do. There is only one of you in the entire cosmos that has walked every single step you have on the Red Road of awakening, and there will only ever be one of you. Sure, your soul carries the codes and memories of all your past and future lives, however there will never be this same you that exists right now, ever again. You are a living, breathing work of art that only has one original copy.

Universal Source Consciousness is getting to view the world through your radiant eyes, learning and expanding from your lived experiences. Essentially, the God Consciousness that lives within you is learning from you, because you have never existed before, thus all the possibilities in your life are new and precious. Your human self is teaching your infinite self what it's like to be you. When you make mistakes or navigate self doubt, it's helpful to remember your innocent and precious cosmic child that lives within. This may open you up to grace and self compassion.

WORTHINESS

Value and worth are inextricably linked, and are ultimately subjective concepts. What one person finds valuable, another may deem frivolous. When we're alchemizing our Metal Element, we are increasing our perception of self worth, unplugging from the conditioned programs of what society has taught us holds value, and tapping back into the innate preciousness that lives within.

Because value and worth are subjective, your ideas, beliefs, opinions and perceptions are not going to be considered valuable to everyone. Let's say growing up you valued artistic expression and wanted to become a poet but your parents valued mathematics and science. You may have grown up devaluing your talents and shrinking your sense of self worth because what you loved and found valuable wasn't received by those around you. The people/society we grew up around plays a huge role in our sense of self worth, as we begin shaping and molding our identity around the things we value from childhood through adolescence.

When we're struggling with self worth, it is helpful to unplug from the mass opinions of the world and attune back to the language of your heart, body and soul. What do you find valuable? As best you can, give yourself permission to pursue the things you find worthy of your time and energy. Surrounding yourself with people who have the same values can also create a positive feedback loop of generating a stronger sense of self worth.

WHAT IF GRIEF BECAME YOUR TEACHER?

"Detachment means letting go and nonattachment means simply letting be."
- Stephen Levine

As we sat in sacred circle at my Tantra training, I watched a fellow peer wail a song from her heart that penetrated up through the temple ceiling, into the heavens above. Kneeling, she kept her heart open, arms outstretched wide, as she bellowed a cry from the base of her womb. Through her trembling voice she called out to her dad – her energy being sent across time and space – asking him why. Why did he still perpetuate the same patterns that hurt her so deeply as a child? Why did he no longer care for himself anymore? Why was he smoking cigarettes and sabotaging his body so soon after a cancer diagnosis? Why was he giving up on life when he had an entire family to tend to? *Why? Why? Why?*

She courageously was a *yes* to doing a group demonstration and allowed us all to witness a tender moment of her diving deep into the well of her Grief. Her questions aptly fit the moment, as what we were doing was a somatic exercise called *Why God*.

In this somatic practice, you come onto your knees and open your heart wide, looking up to the sky with arms open to the sides. It's an energetic replication of the moments in life that literally or energetically take you to your knees. As you do so, you welcome in the moment that is causing you Grief and allow the questions, dialogue, exclamations and body pulsations move through you on all layers – energetic, emotional, physical and spiritual. The key is to keep the heart open as much as you can, even when you want to shut down and close up.

I realized as I watched her cry that her Grief was layered over the very fabric of time. Upon learning the news of her father's cancer diagnosis, she wasn't just grieving for herself in the present moment – a daughter in her mid thirties whose life is about to change through the impending shifts that will come caring for a parent who is ill. She was simultaneously grieving her inner child and the unresolved resentment that younger self, born from her upbringing. Stretching the opposite way across the spiral of time, she was also grieving for her future – imagining her father no longer around.

As I sat and witnessed her in her raw, primal form speaking her heart's truth in one of the most beautifully authentic ways I've ever seen, I saw so much of my previous pain from eight years ago, upon the diagnosis of my dad's cancer, reflected back to me in her story. I also felt ancestral ripples, as my maternal grandfather, once an avid smoker, passed from lung cancer. During that exercise, as a bystander I cried tears of Grief with her. I wondered if my parents were brought to their knees with the pain they felt when their fathers passed.

Resting underneath Grief lay a myriad of complex

emotions that vary from person to person and are transient from moment to moment within each person. Regret. Guilt. Shame. Embarrassment. Rage. Joy. Nostalgia. Sadness. Despair. All of these contextual essences of Grief may have danced their way through your internal landscape as you processed the loss of someone or something.

As this woman allowed us to witness her process, she danced her way through many Emotions, but after some time of plunging into her Grief, she only found Love. After she was able to process her resentment, despair and rage, a natural and spontaneous unfolding of Love spilled out from her. She began connecting the dots of her father's life with her knowledge of Traditional Chinese Medicine.

Every Element connects with physical and energetic parts of the body called the Organs. Partway through her somatic release, she remembered reading that Grief affects the Lungs. She began to see that perhaps her father smoked for the many years of his life as an unconscious way to bring energy into his Lungs from his own Grief he experienced in his life. I was transported back to the story of my grandfather, who drove in his motorcycle behind my grandmother, witnessing their car get into a fatal accident, killing his five year old son. That moment altered his entire life. My pop pop later transitioned from lung cancer, possibly a byproduct of his Grief.

From a spiritual perspective – which means when we look at life experiences looking for meaning that arises from a higher power – underneath Grief there is Love. The reason why Grief pains our hearts as much as it does is because we valued something so greatly, and it is gone. We are reminded, on an unconscious level, just how much that person, experience, pet or life possibility meant to us.

Because the topic of losing a loved one or pet is so

complex, I do wish to add a nuance to this next section. This is a reminder that you cannot feel Grief, or any other Emotion for that matter, wrong. This chapter not only includes our relationship to losing a loved one, but also the symbolism of death that we face all the time, adapting to life's changes and fluctuations.

TRAUMAS THAT SHAPE GRIEF

Below is a brief list of various traumas that could impact the development of your Metal Element, which in turn affects the harmonious expression of Grief.

- Rejection
- Abandonment
- Shaming
- Betrayal
- Cold environment without love
- Abuse from Father Figure
- Unacknowledged grief, caretakers grief
- Divorce
- Loss of a loved one
- Sexual or physical abuse

PHYSICAL, EMOTIONAL + MENTAL MANIFESTATIONS

Below is a brief list of possible physical, emotional and mental issues that can manifest from a dysregulated Metal Element.

- Lung or Heart issues
- Addiction to smoking
- Issues of Large Intestine, constipation

- Tension between shoulder blades
- Asthma, allergies
- Pain in chest, difficulty breathing, shallow breath
- Bronchitis, pneumonia
- Immune system issues
- Skin issues
- Hoarding disorder
- Antisocial personality disorder
- Depression, sadness, isolation, loneliness
- Fear of intimate relationships
- Low self worth
- Jealousy
- Seeking external affirmation
- Hoarding
- Dogmatic beliefs, righteousness
- Obsession with achievements
- Perfectionism, overly critical

Note: *This list is inspired by Traditional East Asian Medicine, Ayurveda and Tantrik Yoga Philosophy.*

PRACTICES THAT ALCHEMIZE EMPATHY

- Present moment awareness practices
- Breathwork Practices (pranayama)
- Building an altar
- Inner child healing
- Maturing inner father archetype
- Mindfulness
- Self Worth Practices
- Embodiment of Primal Self
- Journaling

- Doubling devotional practice
- Connecting with a higher power
- Connecting with spirit guides
- Connecting with highest self
- Gratitude practices
- Meditation
- Forgiveness (Ho'oponopono)

ALCHEMY OF INNER AUTUMN

"Life is now. There was never a time when your life was not now, nor will there ever be."
- Eckhart Tolle

What happens in autumn is a fascinating display of Mother Earth's intelligence. As the daylight fades and the nights grow longer, access to life-giving sunshine diminishes and perennial plants like trees have to adapt to the loss of this life force. With less sunshine, it means there is less chlorophyll production, slowing down over autumn until production eventually ceases. This process is a slow one, happening over time, all the while putting on a dazzling display of color changes.

Every autumn is uniquely different from the last, with some years having unforgettable displays of color and brilliance. Both soil moisture and air temperature affect what hues the leaves actually end up displaying, once their chlorophyll is expended. With an infinite amount of variations of day to day temperatures and soil moisture, it's safe to say that no autumn is ever the same.

Inner Autumn is ruled by the Metal Element, which represents that within you that is valuable and precious. During times of hardship, what keeps me going is remembering how precious all of my life experiences are. All of my perceived mistakes were important data for Source Consciousness to learn, and were never really mistakes to the soul. My increasing sense of self worth comes from acknowledging the very paradox that is me: a limitless, universal consciousness that is connected to all life and can manifest any desire I dream of, while simultaneously being a human being, susceptible to conditioning and social pressure, adapting to inner illusions that filter my reality, sometimes in ways that I allow to cause me hurt.

When I welcome my Infinite Self to communicate with my human self, a portal of self love naturally opens. It is intrinsically difficult to train the ego to fall in love with itself when one has been conditioned into a life of low self worth. However the Infinite Self can and always will love the conditioned self. It's like tapping into a reservoir of endless peace, rather than trying to reroute a river for nourishment.

Inner Autumn's alchemy includes building a relationship with the Higher Self, Spirit Guides and maturing your Inner Father archetype. Just as you hold an Inner Mother, able to provide nourishment and support to yourself, you can embody an Inner Father figure, able to provide praise, acknowledgement and reminders of your worthiness, simply by existing as a precious child of this Universe.

When you engage with Inner Autumn's Emotional Teacher of Grief and explore this Season's alchemical practices, you are able to receive the gifts of this season, namely: Forgiveness, Self Worth and Liberation.

FORGIVENESS

Many spiritual traditions, such as the Ho'oponopono of Hawaii, discuss the importance of forgiveness for a fulfilling alchemical practice. Forgiveness is a multifaceted and often tender exploration of the past, where we may need to revisit unresolved Emotions like Fear, Anger or Grief. When I am cultivating forgiveness (whether for another or for myself) and it feels hard to come by, I double my devotional practice until I have the capacity to forgive.

Doubling your devotion means spending more time in prayer, meditation, embodiment or communion with your spiritual self. Choosing meditations that connect you to your Highest Self, Spirit Guides or Source Consciousness can create a spontaneous and direct line of communication to Universal Love, the field where forgiveness arises from.

Your Highest Self is the part of you that is connected to our divine nature and is always seeking your highest good. When you connect with this aspect of you, you can more easily tap into a deep well of wisdom and compassion that can guide you on our forgiveness. By accessing this higher perspective, you can begin to see yourself with greater compassion and understanding, and to release the self-judgment and shame that may be perpetuating a loop of limiting beliefs. Part of the Alchemy of Inner Autumn is to bring these different parts of you online: your primal/human self plus your Highest Self.

I wonder what would happen for you if you had your Highest (infinite) Self nurture and love upon your human (imperfect) self during times of self doubt, guilt and shame. Yes, you are human. Yes, you make mistakes. And you are also a multifaceted omnipresent beacon of love, just waiting to nurture and hold your human self through anything. Self-forgiveness is not a one-time event, but a process of ongoing self-reflection, acceptance, and release. It requires a willingness to confront your mistakes and take responsibility for your actions with unwavering compassion.

On a meta level, how can you see your active participation in your life, even for the times you believed someone else caused you harm? If it's someone else's fault why you feel a certain way, or if you're continuously attached to the need for someone to be right and another to be wrong, it limits access to your sense of empowerment and ownership of your life. Forgiveness, whether it be for another or yourself, sets you free.

ALCHEMICAL PRACTICE FOR FORGIVENESS: WRITING A CLEARING LETTER

Before jumping to forgiveness, we have to go through a process of feeling the pain from any injustices, harm or pain you believe someone else caused you. The alchemical tool of writing a clearing letter can create a container for you to feel your emotions and acknowledge them. This letter will not actually be shared with the other person. It is for you.

- Write a letter to someone that you've had conflict with. Share your unfiltered perspective of how you're feeling. Don't hold back. Say anything you wish you could say without repercussions.
- As you write, feel the Emotions that arise for you. Consider playing music that matches your energy. Maybe it's something like Rage Against The Machine or music that expresses your emotional undercurrent.

- Pause as needed to do any emotional release techniques (like hand screams or pillow thrashing*). Be sure to take off all jewelry.
- Write until you come to a state of completion and have nothing additional to say.
- Burn or shred this letter when you're ready to release the charge. Full moons are potent times to burn things like clearing letters.

Note #1: *Clients who are enrolled in my Awaken The Divine Feminine mentorship program often write clearing letters as an energetic step of letting go of old relationships. Oftentimes it's done with exes, parents, siblings and old friendships. Sometimes, they do desire to give the letters to the person. For this intention, I teach a three step process of writing drafts. The first draft is the no filter, no holds barred version that does not go to the person. This draft eventually gets burned in a ritual that's in their online course portal. The second draft is revised using certain techniques to omit manipulation language or anything that could be perceived as harmful language. The third draft is one that comes from "I" statements with empowered language. They share this draft with me and we edit it together, so that it can be received by the recipient with intention. These letters can be written to people who are alive, or have transitioned.*

Note #2: *If you want to learn how to practice emotional release techniques safely and effectively, head to the book's website under the Inner Autumn section.*

SELF WORTH

Many of us struggle with feelings of inadequacy, self-doubt, and low self-esteem. In the path of Tantra, it is said that this is an ingrained part of our human self. This nagging feeling that we're somehow unworthy oftentimes initiates a process of self discovery. When the density of feeling unworthy becomes too much, we seek our way back to our infinite nature, where we inevitably remember that we were whole to begin with. We are all divine creations, worthy of love, respect, and compassion. Our worth is not determined by external factors such as success, wealth, or popularity, but by our intrinsic value as both human and multidimensional beings.

Psychologically, self-worth is shaped by our experiences and perceptions of ourselves and the world around us. Our upbringing, relationships, and societal norms can all influence our sense of self-worth, for better or for worse. If you grew up around people who did not value the same things you did, then you may have programming or filters over your self-perception, clouding your ability to see your inherent worth.

This is where the importance of cultivating belonging comes into play. Turn to your soul family, or manifest them, so they can reflect back to you your worth on the days you forget. By connecting with others who value and appreciate you, you can reinforce the subconscious beliefs about yourself and feel more confident in your worth. Even deeper – and perhaps more profoundly – turn to your Spirit Guides for help, guidance and affirmation. Double your devotion so your Highest Self has the portal to communicate with you and love upon your human self, reminding you of your inherent worth.

ALCHEMICAL PRACTICE FOR SELF WORTH: TALK TO YOUR GUIDES AND YOUR UNIVERSAL SELF

Your Universal Self, also known as your Highest Self, is the part of you that only knows the language of Love. They are a part of you and are always looking out for your highest good. Your Highest Self communicates to you through intuitive pings. Building a relationship with your Highest Self is simple. Listen to the intuitive pings that you get and follow through with them. On the other side may be the wisdom you're seeking. My Highest Self often communicates with me on walks in nature or just after exercising. I find that the line of communication is strongest when I'm present, grounded and paying attention to how I feel. You can enjoy guided meditations on free apps like Insight Timer that can teach you how to communicate with this part of you easier.

Connecting with your Spirit Guides is similar, in that you need to feel relaxed and present to hear them. Your guides are on a higher dimension than your worries, so if you're high, drunk, hungover, disembodied or frantic, it's hard to hear them. It's like you're tuned to two different radio stations. It's always a good idea, when connecting with your Highest Self or your Spirit Guides, to find a relaxing state first. Your Spirit Guides may be ancestors, Ascended Masters, Angels, animals, plants, the spirit of Mother Earth, future versions of you (your inner crone), etc. What's even more fun to think about is that all of these things *are* you. All sentient life is animated by the law of One – one Source Consciousness breathing life into many many forms. In essence, the guidance you receive from your guides is coming from you. Check out my Insight Timer profile via the book's website to enjoy a meditation to connect with your guides. (The book's website is www. carleenalarayoga.com/the-akashic-alchemist | password: Alchemist999).

Turning to your Spirit Guides and Higher Self during times of low self worth and self doubt is a transformational process. You'll spontaneously feel the abundant love that washes around you on all sides. Just as parts of you love helping someone else when they're going through a tough time, your Highest Self and Guides *love* showing up to support you. All you need to do is ask!

LIBERATION

Cultivating liberation – or freedom – is an embodied practice, meaning your nervous system, fascia, Heart and soul *feels* free. It is not a cognitive practice. The alchemical path to freedom is usually a process of letting go. Let me say first that I truly loathe the general statement 'let it go' because it reminds me of spiritual bypassing. What I mean here is that letting go is a somatic experience. In order to forgive and let go, we have to first feel the Emotions that are underlying our hurt. In order to let go of limiting beliefs (which are subconscious, meaning they live in the body) we need to cultivate a somatic or embodiment practice of doing rituals designed to safely explore these emotional patterns and reprogram them with new, supportive beliefs on a cellular level. Finding true freedom means using your *body* rather than your brain to do the alchemy.

I see many clients who are frustrated after years of talk therapy because they aren't seeing the sustainable liberation from old patterns and emotional loops as they desire. This is not throwing shade on psychotherapy, but illuminating a need to have supplemental practices that bridge the gap between the cognitive mind and the feeling based body. We need more holistic approaches that address the somatic body (your nervous system and fascia) which is where your emotions actually live. Freedom lives somewhere within your mind-body connection.

ALCHEMICAL PRACTICE FOR LIBERATION: SOMATIC RELEASE EXERCISES

Liberation is generating Emotional freedom from the burden of your past and the worries of the future. This includes letting go of old emotions/stuck energy that live in your energy field. In my Awaken the Divine Feminine Mentorship, I guide my clients through specific emotional release techniques like hand screams, pillow thrashing, Why God grief release, aspecting and more. We focus on bringing the Emotions of Anger or Grief online in the body. This creates a pulse of life force that can be used for prayer, manifestation, liberation and letting go. Emotional release techniques are at the foundation of the work I do with clients who are wanting to taste, touch and feel true freedom in this lifetime. There's a great YouTube video on the book's website to learn more about this alchemical tool.

ALCHEMICAL TOOLS FOR INNER AUTUMN

The Inner Alchemy process that occurs during Autumn will bring online your Inner Father Archetype. This is the part of you that acknowledges your growth, celebrates your wins, offers praise and believes in your capability for change and manifestation. Just as we activate our Inner Mother in The Space Between, we are met with the support of the Inner Father during Autumn. While doing any of the alchemical practices this Season, set the intention that you're bringing your most encouraging, supportive and active Inner Father into the picture.

- Present moment awareness practices
- Breathwork practices (pranayama)
- Building an altar
- Inner child healing
- Maturing inner father
- Mindfulness practices
- Self Worth Practices
- Somatic Release Exercises
- Hypnotherapy
- Yin Yoga
- Mantra meditation
- Processing Grief
- Embodiment of Primal Self
- Journaling
- Doubling devotional practice
- Connecting with a higher power
- Connecting with spirit guides
- Connecting with highest self
- Gratitude practices
- Meditation
- Forgiveness (Ho'oponopono)

CYCLE SIX: INTEGRATION

INTEGRATION

*"In many shamanic societies, if you came to a medicine person
complaining of being disheartened, dispirited, or depressed, they would
ask one of four questions:
'When did you stop dancing?
When did you stop singing?
When did you stop being enchanted by stories?
When did you stop being comforted by the sweet territory of silence?'"*
- Gabrielle Roth

I'd like to acknowledge and celebrate you for navigating the Akashic Alchemist Wheel of the Year, traveling through Inner Winter, Spring, Summer, The Space Between, and Autumn! I invite you to take a moment of self reflection and to celebrate this journey. Whether you've read the book straight through or hopped around across stretches of time. Whether you tried some of the alchemical practices or not. What an amazing feat that you've invested time, energy and love into your soul by exploring the path of *The Akashic Alchemist*.

While channeling this book, my guides and Mother

Earth made it clear that there needed to be a section called Integration, as a sweet reprieve from the growth, inner work and expansion. A time for self acknowledgement! I wonder how often you afford yourself acknowledgement? I wonder how many times a year you pause between the manifesting, healing and transformation to give yourself permission to be exactly where you are? If there's one thing I've noticed in my clients – which are amazing mirrors to me – is that we can get stuck in what I call the transformation trap, forever caught on the hamster wheel of spiritual growth.

The transformation trap is when you believe that there is always something to fix about yourself, caught in a feedback loop of incessant self-discovery without pausing to celebrate how far you've come. It's actually one of the shadows of the Scorpio astrological archetype: being addicted to transformation. Self growth, development and expansion are important for your soul, your family and humanity. *And* it's just as important to put down the "work" and integrate.

Perhaps this transformation trap came up while reading this book. As you digest all of this information, notice if you're feeling like there's still "so much to do." Here is a loving reminder to that part of self: the teachings in this book are intended to be a living breathing resource for you to turn to when you need grounded tools. They are not a prescriptive program that must all be undertaken, as not all the tools will be relevant to your Inner Alchemy and life experiences.

As you Integrate, give yourself permission to take your time digesting, and remember that you are whole. When all parts of self come together to live in a harmonious and right relationship together, you have arrived at Integration. Integration means *to make whole*, and is of paramount importance within this journey. I'd like to add a nuance to the definition of integration, because you already *are* whole. This phase is about remembering this.

I find integration and remember my inherent wholeness in the precious moments of stillness when I meditate. I remember it when I walk among rustling trees, bare feet on moss. I smell it in banana bread baked by someone who loves me. I taste it in a ripe yellow dragon fruit. I tap into it when I ecstatically dance.

Sometimes we can flit from book to book, course to course, training to training, hoping that this next thing will bring the integration we seek, forgetting that it can be in the simplest moments. In the early years after my great awakening of 2012 I felt that I was always running out of time, feeling like my neurons may explode from just how deep the alchemical rabbit hole could go. Oh, how much self work needed to be done! Inner child healing. Teenage years. Past lives. Multiple timelines. Alternate dimensions. Extraterrestrial life. Shadow work. Spirit guides. *Am I even making a dent?!*

This ruthless scramble of believing I was someone to fix, always having some place to catch up to, never arriving, was like I had become a mad scientist. A mad scientist is always tweaking – never satisfied with the results – always squeezed from the inevitable passage of time. Inversely, an alchemist receives information as it comes in, synthesizes it and trusts when the big picture has not been revealed yet. The alchemist works with what is and enjoys the process, curiously exploring the wondrous world around them. The alchemist is not transforming an uncomfortable emotion into something else – they are transforming their *relationship* to what is, so that the emotion can be seen as holy, divine and supportive. The difference is: the mad scientist thinks there is some code to crack and something to figure out, while the alchemist feels that all is unfolding in divine perfection and the quest is discovering more of how that could be true. The mad scientist is trying to fix themself and the world. The alchemist is remembering that there is nothing to fix, only more to Love.

Out of all that I've learned from being a mad scientist and alchemist alike, my biggest takeaway is that I have all I am seeking. Feeling my Emotions through alchemical practices like breathwork, meditation, dance, somatic practices, connecting to the Earth and embodiment have opened up a treasure trove of wisdom that sat within my, untapped.

You may have found that across your lifetime there have been experiences that have not yet been integrated into your alchemical toolbox. Perhaps there are moments in time that feel frozen in place, or they are unconsciously hidden away for now. Mysterious moments that yet to have meaning sit in the cosmic closet of your soul, untouched. Honoring the phase of Integration includes trusting that you do not have to crack yourself open and aggressively explore the depths for healing. Such an exploration happens spontaneously and in divine timing and only when your nervous systems feel ready to integrate. This is a process that happens in accordance with cosmic time.

Sometimes it takes months or even years to fully digest a significant life experience, such as after attending a continuing education program or yoga teacher training, for example. Other times our metabolization process may be shorter, lasting a few days or weeks. In either circumstance, there comes a time when an overwhelming amount of information just begins to make *sense*. This is integration.

If you're reading this book, you've most likely done some work on yourself in some way shape or form. This chapter is designed to not only apply as support for when you're navigating your inner Seasons, but to offer guidance and tools to support Integration after any type of major life experience such as returning from a plant medicine ceremony, finishing an online course, or graduating from a yoga teacher training. What we're missing in many spiritual circles is the support that comes "after" something significant has come to completion. It is my hope that these tools are like a compass for you when you're integrating from any life initiation.

TEN ALCHEMICAL TOOLS FOR INTEGRATION

After completing a training, course or transformational book, consider that that is when the real training starts. When you go out into the real world, view your outer reality like a cosmic sandbox for your soul to play, learn and grow. Put the practices you learned into action. Consciously choose to ooze compassion and embody presence for the best results. When you're integrating:

1. **Be mindful of your consumption.** You've just ingested a tremendous amount of information! Give yourself time to digest. This metabolic process may take days, weeks and sometimes years, depending on the journey. Ask yourself, do I really need to add more right now, or am I full?

2. **Be mindful of social media.** In the precious hours that follow expansive things like reading a soul-expanding book, attending events like ecstatic dances or full/new moon circles or graduating from trainings, your energy field is wide open and your subconscious

is like a sponge. Use discernment with what you fill it with.

3. **Stay connected to yourself**. Prioritize your morning or evening practice and self care time to stay connected to you. Let this be nonnegotiable.

4. **Rest.** Your body has been hard at work feeding your brain and Heart energy. You deserve time to recalibrate. Rest helps rewire the nervous system, unwinds the fascial matrix and is your superpower to rejuvenate your energy reserves. Rest also gives you space to reflect upon what you learned.

5. **Don't close down.** When we go through spiritual initiations, we attune our sensitivity to the world in a significant way. You are more connected to yourself and others than ever before. This can feel overwhelming at first as you feel the pulse of the world again. This is normal. It may also feel disheartening to know that you've done the work and perceive that your loved ones around you haven't. Trust their process. Embody yours. Keep your heart open and don't close down.

6. **Wait before making big decisions.** When we do alchemical work, we may come to earth-shattering realizations. Give yourself at least a lunar cycle (twenty-eight days) to journal or meditate upon big decisions like ending a relationship, moving, changing jobs, etc. Unless something is threatening your immediate safety and well-being, give your realizations time to settle and make a wise plan that keeps your nervous system's health in mind.

7. **Practice radical discontinuity.** Radical discontinuity is when you consciously choose to break out of your routine. Brush your teeth with the opposite hand. Get out of bed on the opposite side. Rearrange the steps you do to make your morning coffee or tea. Every time you practice radical discontinuity, your brain is being primed with new neural networks. This creates an alchemical window where you can reflect on all you learned and integrate it into your subconscious.

8. **Nurture your physical body.** Receive body work like massage or acupuncture, spend time in nature, continue with your embodiment practices like yoga, dance or exercise. These are all ways to keep the mind-body connection open. It will also support you during the inevitable ups and downs of integration.

9. **Own who you are.** When you read books with new information or attend trainings that stretch the capacity of your mind, you may be grappling with conflicting ideas. Remember that your spiritual practice is exactly that: *yours*. Take time to journal on what aspects/ beliefs/ perspectives you want to keep, which ones you put on a shelf to revisit later and which you entirely throw away. Own your Truth.

10. **Share about what you learned.** Journal, blog or spark up a conversation with a friend. One of the best ways we can integrate new information is to practice teaching it!

REMEMBER WHO YOU ARE

*"…with the infinite options available to Her,
Consciousness chose to become you."*
- Christopher D. Wallis

Within every human being lives a stargate capable of transporting you into the realm of infinite possibilities. Every thought, a quantum impulse that is ready and willing to become something and anything. Every desire, a spark that can manifest things into form. Every feeling is a sacred teacher that has arrived to teach you more about yourself. Deep within the center of your earthly matter you hold vast void spaces of creation, death, transformation and rebirth.

Your physical form is an embodied temple composed of the same elements, minerals and mind-bending particles that coalesced to create the visible Universe. In essence, you *are* a walking, living, breathing Universe that is continuously creating, sustaining, destroying and rebirthing oneself – a process that happens inside of your body trillions of times a day within the trillions of cells that make up your physical form, like magick.

When we zoom out to the macrocosm of this multiverse, we see patterns emerge. All of the cosmos is in a cyclical dance of expansion and contraction, unfurling and exploding only to ebb and retract inward, dying and rebirthing once again. The cycle continues on. In the deepest depths of winter we know that summer will come again, just as we know the sun will continue to rise. There is a time for full, unbounded expression, just as there is a time to symbolically die.

This transient dance of changing states is ironically the only constant we know. So why is it that we put so much pressure on ourselves to be one way all the time? In nature it isn't feasible for flowers to bloom all year round or for all trees to hold onto their leaves and never let go. We see that death always brings life. We see the unique and multifaceted expressions of all life that are intricately connected and dazzlingly unique.

Our ancient ancestors once lived in harmony with these changing states of life Herself, attuned to the Earth and the cosmos alike. We once worshiped our Emotions as sacred teachers and if we were struggling, we chose embodiments like dance, song, or emotional release to unleash stagnant energy and feel the most tender depths of what it means to be human. We worked together understanding that we co-regulate one another's nervous systems without words even needing to be said.

May we remember the ancient value of living in right relationship with one another, living in small communities, tending to our land, making wise and discerning choices for a sustainable future while reveling in the entirety of the complex human emotional spectrum. This way, the way of all ancient cultures on Earth for hundreds of thousands of years worked, and it worked well.

When we live in harmony with all parts of self, with others and with the land, life begins to click into place. Instead of wondering, "*why am I still dealing with this pattern? I thought I fixed this,*" we see the returning theme as a loving reminder that the Universe is co-creating with you. A cyclical dance across the fabric of time, that each time something "old" returns back to you, it has already decayed, died and was reborn again – every moment is anew.

The alchemist delights when something "old" arrives again, as the Alchemist curiously asks themself, "*what do I want to do with this now? How sweetly can I tend to myself and my inner landscape?*"

If you ever feel as though you are going in circles, it is because you are! Yet those circles are actually loops upon a cosmic spiral that is always evolving and expanding outward. Remember this the next time you feel you're going backwards. Time and life's evolution happens like a fibonacci spiral, that at times it appears we are in retrograde.

There may be moments when you are in your Divine Masculine Shadow, defending against life. Others you may be internalizing life's experiences in the Divine Feminine Shadow. We've come to a realm with the illusion of duality so that we can learn from these different polarities. No time is ever wasted, even when you are in your Shadow, because life is a sweet harmonious dance of both. Wisdom and alchemical gold live in the Shadow realm and the rainy months/days/years are just as precious as the sunshine.

RE-INDIGENIZE YOUR
RELATIONSHIP WITH THE EARTH

"For all of us, becoming Indigenous to a place means living as if your children's future mattered, to take care of the land as if our lives, both material and spiritual, depended on it."
- Robin Wall Kimmerer

At the time of publishing this book I will be halfway through a four year initiation with the Mexica people of México. Every October, under the full hunter's moon in October, hundreds of women gather to sing, dance, shed, transmute, heal and pray for the evolution of humanity. Each year I learn more about their culture, the land, the Elements, my ancestors, my lineage and about humanity.

On the third day of ceremony in 2022 I was drifting in and out of lucid states as I sat in my tent. I pulled out my journal, feeling the sacred land of Teotihuacán wanting to speak to me. Because I was bleeding, I was even more perceptive to channeling – our moon cycles being times when women are their most oracle-like. Coming in clear as the moon that shone above us the night before, I was asked by some mysterious Spirits if the first word of the book could be the word 'Indigenous.' At the time, I didn't know *what* the Introduction of the book would be, but it felt right to honor this request. I listened and obliged because I felt in my bones that it was important.

Months later, as I wrap up the writing of this book, I see now *why* that request was asked. It was a request that spiraled up from the depths of the sacred land of Teotihuacán, from all of the Indigenous tribes that have tended to the soil long before I arrived. The request also came from the living pulse alive within my ethereal DNA of my own Indigenous ancestors. Placing the energy of 'Indigenous' right at the beginning was to be a call to action for all of us: it is time to place our Indigenous roots back at the forefront of our way of life, so that we can restore our right relationship to the Earth of our bodies, and in turn to the Earth of our Great Mother. Our species cannot sustain itself if we don't.

For hundreds of thousands of years, humanity was Indigenous. To be Indigenous means to steward, or to care for, our land and ensure that harmony and reciprocity is embodied and valued. To live in reciprocity with the land means being mindful of how much we take, and spending just as much time or energy in giving.

For hundreds of thousands of years ancient cultures from all over the world, up until 3,500 years ago, looked towards the Earth in reciprocal worship. Prayer was held in caves. Sorrow and Fear were released into the oceans to be carried away by the tides. Grief tumbled out from our Hearts and down into the soil, to be composted back to us as Love. Our sacred Rage was a primal pleasure energy that activated all of our energy centers and created change. Joy rippled up from the simplest of moments, from hearing the locusts hum in the forests or witnessing the sky change from blue to cotton candy purple. Gifts in the form of seeds, flowers and smoke were offered back to the Earth, held in the package of gratitude.

Somewhere, across the passage of time, there grew a fissure between us and our Great Mother. Colonization swept across the globe, severing all of our ancestors from our culture while most significantly harming those who did not fit into the dominant power structure. Greed and quests for power replaced gratitude and quests for peace as we entered into a dark age. We moved away from worshiping the Earth and our internal sense of Source Consciousness towards worshiping ideologies that were outside of ourselves.

At the time this book came to me, I had been walking just about every day for a year. A simple walk that stretched two blocks in every direction around my home. After some time I began to notice things I never noticed before. I heard the owls' calls across the bare trees, rippling frequencies of wisdom through my window in winter. I noticed that spring brought our entire neighborhood a bouquet of flowers that lasted for weeks. In summer I was awed by the scraps of sycamore bark all over my neighbors' yards, inspiring a curiosity to learn more about why. In autumn I went on epic scavenger hunts, finding mushrooms camouflaged amongst the leaves. My little witch of the woods that lived within my heart, who I hadn't seen since childhood, emerged again. I started making potions again, this time in the form of tinctures and herbal teas as I dove deep into plant medicine. Slowly, I was finding my way home again, to being a child, a student of this great Earth, who is innocent, whole and pure. There came a particular day when I began believing in magick again, sparked from the brilliance of noticing the fireflies. It had been decades since I'd acknowledged their familiar brilliance, but they hadn't gone anywhere.

The average American spends 90% of their time indoors.[1] How can we ever come to revere the very Earth that gives us life if we never come to visit her and experience her gifts, her magick and her bounty first-hand? How can we return to that child-like state, caught in wonder and daydreaming of a perfect world, if we do not allow ourselves to explore, play and learn? We forget that the water we drink that nourishes our cells, the food we eat that sustains our energy and the clothing we wear that protects us from the elements comes from Her. We forget that we are surrounded in endless abundance, with enough for every single person on this planet, and counting. We forget that all of our troubles could be offered up to her, so that she can compost them and recycle that energy for better use. We forget that by placing our bare feet upon her grass or placing our hands on the trunk of her trees bio-electromagnetically replenishes us from the quantum level up to the physical level.[2] Please do not let the conditioning of popular culture trick you into believing this is hippy-dippy and woo-woo. Spending time in, around and with the Earth heals you – this fact is grounded in science *and* Indigenous wisdom.

With all of this, I invite you into the final initiation of *The Akashic Alchemist*. To take this ancient wisdom and put it into aligned and inspired action. The Sanskrit word *dharma* means fulfilling your purpose while enjoying your highest form of joy. We all have come here with our particular spice, flavor and texture of how we'd like to support the rising of consciousness on this planet. In lieu of this, I'd like to suggest some options of how you can re-indigenize your relationship to your cosmic home, to restore harmony within yourself, your community and to support future generations to come. It may feel overwhelming to tackle it all, so choose the tools that light you up and build from there.

ALCHEMICAL TOOLS FOR RE-INDIGENIZING YOUR RELATIONSHIP TO THE EARTH

- Compost or eliminate as much of your food waste as possible. According to the Food and Agriculture Organization of the United Nations, food loss and waste is "a global problem of enormous economic, environmental and societal significance."[3] Food waste (like fruit/vegetable scraps, coffee grounds and eggshells) sits in landfills and cannot be broken down properly. This leads to significant emissions of methane which is eighty times more harmful than carbon dioxide towards climate change.[4] Through composting, you significantly reduce these emissions from your household and create beautiful soil that can be put to better use. Many towns have composting services, such as Garden State Composting in my home area of Southern New Jersey.
- When planting your garden, ensure you include wildflowers and plants that attract pollinators (like bees and butterflies). Our food supply relies on healthy and sustainable regeneration of pollinators.
- In autumn, leave the leaves! Leaves are an integral part of the pollinator ecosystem. Caterpillars, lizards, birds, turtles, pollinators and other critters overwinter in the leaves. Mass

removal for the sake of a perfect lawn disrupts the food chain significantly.[5] The healthy decay of leaves also adds nutrients into the soil, removing the need to add fertilizer come spring. It's interesting to note that the obsession with the perfect lawn came from marketing from big business in the 1950s. They advertised toxic and carcinogenic products that would transform "wild" and "unruly" lawns into perfection. The tame American lawn became a subconscious symbol for success. It's time to unplug from this old program as a loving symbol of resistance against big business, plugging back into Earth wisdom.

- When necessary, if you must cut down a tree (due to old age or hazards), plant two more on your property. If your property is barren of trees, plant some. This will create an entire ecosystem of life, filtering the air you breathe and replenishing groundwater reserves. Not to mention, those trees may be the perfect spot for a future treehouse or swing for little ones in generations to come!

- Avoid using harsh and carcinogenic lawn care treatments like Monstanto's RoundUp. Do your due diligence with all products you use on your lawn, makeup, hair products, and anything that goes into the soil or water such as snow melts, grass seed, weed killers, etc. There are plenty of ways to make your own household items or you can buy local/from online shops from others who hand make them.

- Say no to fast fashion. Most of the microplastics, toxic dyes and chemicals used in fast fashion become absorbed into our skin and are carcinogenic. Most of this clothing (and the scraps) ends up in landfills, and eventually in the oceans and waterways, polluting them.[6] Choose sustainable clothing that you could imagine having for generations to come or thrift.

- Consider eating plant based a few times a week. In the United States, it takes 600 gallons of water – which is like leaving your shower running for 2 months straight – to create one beef hamburger patty.[7]

Now, I must admit, as I write all of this, there is that nagging voice within me that says, *indeed this world is fucked.* But that is not very empowering a place to live, nor is it helpful. The truth is, there are sustainable choices that we can make on a day to day basis that will add up and multiply by the thousands, millions and then billions. Consider that each time you opt for sustainable options, you are living in reciprocal relationship with our planet, sending gratitude through your aligned action. You are an important puzzle piece and have the power to make an impact. We each individually hold a responsibility to tend to this planet. Ambivalence is no longer an option. Apathy is what will kill us.

We *must* make sustainable choices that have future generations in mind as we are approaching a crossroads of change. Re-indigenizing our relationship with this planet is what will tip the scales, shifting us away from imminent ruin via self destruction into harmony and collective (r)evolution. We cannot thrive without tending to the land and the Earth. The benefit to this is that not only will we keep our species alive, but we will be returning back to our ancient ways of learning from this planet, inspiring more abundance, creativity, and connection back to Source Consciousness, which is where our true joy and happiness comes from.

RE-INDIGENIZE YOUR INNER EARTH

Re-indigenizing your inner world means tending to healthy habits/beliefs and giving yourself permission to live in harmony with yourself. The root of the word harmony comes from being in tune with one's cycles.[8] We don't expect the moon to be full all the time, so why do we expect that of ourselves? To live harmoniously means, then, to give yourself permission to have an Inner Winter, Spring, Summer, Late Summer and Autumn. Feel your fluctuating Emotions grounded in compassion. Give yourself permission to ebb and flow just like the tides and the moon, as we all have internal cycles and phases.

Sometimes we flow through cycles that complete in an hour, a day, a week or a month. Sometimes our inner phases last longer. It isn't uncommon for our internal cycles to be different from those in the world around us. You may be navigating an Inner Autumn despite it being summer outside. If you are in tune with your internal rhythms and place your focus and priority on that rhythm rather than contorting yourself to what's outside of you, you are committing an act of self love. Rather than resist your inner cycles, which only makes the underlying energy persist, you can relax and soften into the impermanence of it all: this too shall pass, and for now I will be with what is.

Remind yourself that you belong in your most holy and sacred home: the earth of your body. Your soul is Indigenous to your bones and blood. Foster an unwavering practice of compassion so that you can alchemize your

DNA for future generations to come. Remember that the pain you transmute within yourself is an offering of Love to all of your future family members, and for all of those that surround you now. The more you come home to yourself and remember your abundant power, you serve the awakening of consciousness on our planet.

On the days that you forget who you are, come Home, back to the vessel of your body and back into the playground of this planet. Remember that this was the alchemical way of our ancient ancestors: when we were in doubt, we turned to the Earth and one another.

Hardwired for social connection, we sang, laughed, danced and tended to those around us and the land like the intricately delicate and precious expressions we are, together. Our community was once currency, Our balance was reciprocity. We lived in tribal groups that shared responsibilities amongst one another. We respected and revered our elders. We gathered in ceremonies, song and prayer often. We observed the transits of the cosmos using mathematical equations, studying patterns which amplified our power from working in harmony with the relationship between the Earth and the cosmos.

Your Indigenous ancestors knew the songs of the plants in their native areas and knew to never take more than they needed, planting more as needed for sustainability. Your ancestors had culture, rich with rituals and healing practices. Re-indigenizing your inner world means reclaiming your responsibility over the land you steward, and reclaiming your relationship to your ancestral roots. Your ancestral culture, which may have been stolen from you from colonization and patriarchal domination, may hold the keys to restoring balance back on this planet. Consider looking into your ancestry's alchemical practices and applying them to your life, reclaiming your ancient culture back into your lineage.

Today we see the after-effects of well-designed subconscious programs that continuously feed us distractions to bigger problems – the greatest of which is that our home may not be hospitable for us within our lifetime if we continue down this path. Re-indigenizing your inner world and tending to the land and community around you will mend the wound of separating yourself from nature. Through Inner Alchemy and reconnecting with the Earth, you will remember that you *are* nature. We have not lost our Indigenous and intimate relationship to the Earth, because we are made of her and from her – you are her child. We have just gotten distracted. We were conditioned to be and feel small, no longer believing in our Source Consciousness that pulsed through our very veins. We forgot that we were all interconnected. You still have that Source Consciousness within you. It *is* you.

You are Source Consciousness experiencing itself as you and there will never be another you, alive during this pivotal time. You chose to come. You chose to read this book. You chose to receive this message: the Earth wants you to remember that you already are integrated. Innocent. Empowered. Sovereign. You are important and the work you do during this lifetime is important. May you remember that you are the alchemist, capable of designing the most magickal life. May you remember that your original state is Love.

A CALL TO ACTION

Indigenous peoples across the world are the most invisible, meaning they are often left out of policy making, access to economic funding, education and social services, and have experienced some of the most significant impacts from colonization, eminent domain and systemic injustice.

Globally, they are some of the world's most vulnerable groups. Indigenous peoples make up six percent of the global population yet they represent nineteen percent of the world's impoverished, with many living significantly below the poverty line.[1] They have the highest rates of violence than any other population. Indigenous women are ten times more at risk than any other demographic for rape, murder, violence and abuse. According to the U.S. Department of the Interior for Indian Affairs, in "[a] 2016 study by the National Institute of Justice (NIJ) found that more than four in five American Indian and Alaska Native women (84.3 percent) have experienced violence in their lifetime, including 56.1 percent who have experienced sexual violence."[2] The risk for violence does not only apply

for women, though. A recent study conducted by the NIJ
found that, "[more] than four in five American Indian and
Alaska Native men (81.6 percent) have experienced
violence in their lifetime."[3]

There is – and has been – an urgent need to uplift,
protect and celebrate Indigenous groups, as their rights are
continuing to be violated. Across the globe governments
are still stealing land from tribal groups using eminent
domain in the false mask of nature conservancy. Within
the United States, hundreds of years after the founding of
this country on stolen land, the government continues
similar patterns under the guise of environmental
protection. According to Survival International – an NGO
that works to protect tribal groups' human rights – shares
that, "[evidence] proves indigenous people understand and
manage their environment better than anyone else. 80% of
Earth's biodiversity is in tribal territories and when
indigenous peoples have secure rights over their land, they
achieve at least equal if not better conservation results at a
fraction of the cost of conventional conservation
programs."[4]

The effects of such injustices are undoubtedly
heartbreaking and they deserve a voice. Just as the
heartbreak deserves acknowledgement, so, too does the
wisdom, perseverance, resiliency and expansiveness of
Native culture. I believe in a world where we make our way
back to worshiping the land around us. Where we turn to
this planet as our Great Teacher, mending the heart-fissure
that is created from feeling separate from nature. My
reverence for this planet and all that she has to teach us,
when we take the time to get to know her and commune
with her, comes directly from being a student of
Indigenous, earth-based wisdom.

Advocating for the rights of Native people, educating

ourselves on culture, social responsibility and being allies through our action is imperative. The future relies on our willingness to honor the disparities that have taken place globally, make amends for reparations and ancestral lands returning to Indigenous groups and take action for sustainable and equitable change.

The intention behind this closing chapter is to inspire you to take an interest in becoming more involved with your local communities, becoming an advocate for the Native populations in your area or country. Reading and educating ourselves is certainly an important piece of the puzzle, but what we choose to do with our hearts, minds, hands and actions is even more significant! I invite you, through these calls to action, to take a stand and advocate for Native peoples in your area so we can begin tipping the scales back to equitable frameworks that support all of humanity, rather than the 1 percent.

TAKING ACTION

If you are feeling inspired to take action, I invite you to head to the book's website (link below) and click the 'Inspired Action' tab. This will bring you to a host of resources to choose from that relate to how you can get involved with advocating for social justice and equity.

Book's Website:
www.carleenalarayoga.com/theakashicalchemist
Password: Alchemist999

WHY I ADVOCATE FOR INDIGENOUS RIGHTS

I studied Psychology during my undergrad because I wanted to understand human behavior on a deeper level. I was insatiably curious about why people commit crimes, struggle with things like addiction, and why we were seeing rising rates of anxiety and depression like never before. My perspective was that if I became a psychotherapist, I could impact the world one heart at a time.

While completing my required electives, I was assigned Sociology 101 where I took class with professor Lisa Ruchti at West Chester University. During this class she showed a documentary on the banana trade industry and the effects of colonization, the global economic market and the British Empire on Jamaica. After leaving that class, my future was forever changed. Within me there sparked a burning rage at the complex, global and systemic injustices that were happening all the time, hidden beneath the surface of marketing faces like the Chiquita banana icon. I wanted to be a part of the change and be a peaceful disruptor of the power structures at bay, as I realized that the individual experiences of depression, anxiety and health complications were often symptoms of global systemic injustices. At the time it was too late to change my major to study further, but I reconciled this with continuing my education and studying in a Sociology graduate program.

A month before I was scheduled to live in Queens, NY to study Sociology, my plans changed once again when I discovered by pure chance a Master's program that brought me to five countries to study International Nongovernmental Organizations, or INGOs. This story I tell briefly in the chapter *Keep Your Eyes Focused*. Back in 2014, the INGO program was a subdivision of the International Relations department. Essentially, my studies revolved around social justice, equity and advocacy for marginalized groups that have been disproportionately affected by systemic injustice. I had the privilege to study in

Bangkok Thailand; London, UK; Leiden, Netherlands; Geneva, Switzerland and Washington D.C., USA to understand the global context of such injustices.

My specialization changed a few times, first focusing on global networks of human and sex trafficking, then to studying Indigenous rights and reparations. I eventually landed on writing my Master's thesis on the importance of mindfulness based programs in the educational system, particularly for inner city youth to provide sustainable resources for the United States' most vulnerable populations, which includes Indigenous youth.

During my time in London, UK I was a volunteer for multiple human rights organizations, including Survival International, Amnesty International and supported in orchestrating the annual fundraising gala for Human Rights Watch – an NGO that investigates and publishes on abuses occurring in all corners of the world. When I moved to Geneva, Switzerland I became a volunteer for DOCIP, or the Indigenous Peoples' Center for Documentation, Research and Information and made routine visits to the United Nations offices to study, learn and take notes on the global human rights climate and the blossoming voices that Indigenous groups were advocating for in the United Nations. Since graduating from my M.A., I have continued my passion for social equity in various ways, such as educating on the need for cultural responsibility in the wellness world, spirituality, yoga and in sustainable herbalism.

In addition to my formal training and volunteer work, I have a personal tie to studying human rights as a homage to my Indigenous ancestors. Many of them are on my team of spirit guides that spoke to me in length while writing this book. *Yo soy una mestiza*. *Mestiza* is a word that describes people who have both European and Indigenous

American ancestry. I hold the ancestral codes of the Taino people of the Caribbean, the Bantu of Africa, the blood of various tribes from Panama, Costa Rica, Bolivia, Uruguay and Paraguay, the druids, bards and ovates of Ireland, and the stewards of what is now Scicily. Within my lineage and DNA I hold the energetic imprints of both the colonizer and the colonized. I've heard from my ancestors on both sides of history and have learned much from their guidance, regrets, hardships and wisdom.

What I've learned through my studies and my ancestral connection is that from a micro to a macro global level, Indigenous groups have been systemically removed from their ancestral lands in order for governments, corporations and the worlds 1% to profit off of their resource-rich land, all at the expense of intentionally separating families, engaging in genocide, actively dismantling language and culture, and separating people from their source of connection with Great Spirit, Mother Earth and the Spirits that live within the Water, Wind, Fire and Earth.

The effects of Indigenous genocide and removal of Native peoples' rights to steward their ancestral land has had not only harmful psychological and physiological affects on such groups, but also a grave impact on our environment's health and well-being. Earth-based Indigenous groups were the stewards to their native lands for hundreds of thousands of years and systemic removal of such tribal groups has created harmful environmental impacts in addition to the deplorable psycho socio-emotional implications.

I share this context with you to give you a little pre-history to my intentions why I chose to highlight Indigenous peoples, wisdom and traditions within *The Akashic Alchemist*. It is my dream to one day soon be a part of the returning of ancestral lands, rights and reparations to Indigenous groups worldwide. I see a stark need for Indigenous wisdom to be rewoven back into the collective consciousness for the viability of humanity and to once again make Indigenous art, culture, songs, prayers, philosophies and stories visible once again. The health of our planet and all of our descendants relies upon it.

NOTE: *It is my desire to be culturally responsible and update this book as a living, breathing transmission in future versions to come. If you have feedback or concerns with the social literacy of this version, please send an email to support@theakashicalchemist.com. I am open to suggestions and intend to keep this book updated with socially appropriate information, resources and educational content that respects all cultures, ethnicities, races and demographics. I am also open to collaborating on socially responsible projects that support the mission of returning land and reparations to Native peoples. If you'd like to connect on either of these subjects, send our team an email and we'll be in touch shortly. Thank you.*

GLOSSARY

Akasha [sanskrit] - a universal etheric field or dimension in which a record of all past, present and future events is imprinted, recorded and remembered; ether/space (sanskrit). *Related: **Akashic Records:** the ethereal dimension where all of recorded time is accessible to any living being in the cosmos. Carl Jung called this "supraconsciousness"*

Alchemist - a person who transforms or creates something through inner alchemy processes through aligning oneself with natural forces to manifest an intention

Alchemy - to transform from one state to another through intentional internal processes through aligning oneself with natural forces to manifest an intention

Belonging - an emotional state of feeling safe and included within a group. This safety allows for authentic self expression. Belonging can also apply to one's inner landscape, meaning you allow the different parts of you to belong inside your own psyche.

Divine Feminine - an archetypal energy that is interchangeable to Yin Energy. It is connected to emotion, pleasure, intimacy, creativity, matter, the physical body, Mother Earth, compassion, nurturance, nourishment, trust, and surrender. It has Lunar qualities and is connected to the left side of the body and the right hemisphere of the brain. It has either a neutral, downward or inward movement. It is connected to Inner Winter (Water), The Space Between (Earth) and Inner Autumn (Metal). One of the primary processes of Inner Alchemy is to balance the internal Divine Feminine and Divine Masculine energies within (see divine masculine for more).

Divine Masculine - an archetypal energy that is interchangeable to Yang Energy. It is connected to thought, ideas, inspiration, desire, motivation, safety, presence and awareness. It has Solar qualities and is connected to the right side of the body and the left hemisphere of the brain. It has either an upward or outward movement. It is connected to Inner Spring (Wood) and Inner Summer (Fire). One of the primary processes of Inner Alchemy is to balance the Divine Masculine and Divine Feminine energies within (see Divine Feminine for more)

Dysregulation - when the sympathetic nervous system is either over or under activated and can create unconscious stress state manifestations like freezing, fleeing, fawning, or fighting.

Earth Element - The Earth Element is Divinely Feminine and its direction is neutral. It represents balance, stability, nourishment, physical matter, abundance, your inner mother, ancestral healing. Earth is connected to the Emotion of Empathy, symbolizing your ability to be in reciprocal relationship with others, giving and receiving.

Embodiment - The alchemical process of bringing one's conscious awareness into the felt-sense of the body, generating movement (like dance, yoga, somatic release or breathwork, for example) to process any emotions that may be "frozen" in the tissues of the body. This is a divine feminine form of healing and inner alchemy that can unlock old memories or emotions in order to rewrite new, more helpful narratives and beliefs. Embodiment can be interchangeable with Somatics.

Emotional Teacher - An Emotional Teacher is the archetypal energy that moves through you. When you give yourself permission to feel an Emotion fully, it has a lesson, breakthrough or nugget of wisdom for you on the other side. The alchemical practices in *The Akashic Alchemist* can give you inspiration on how to work with your Emotions in an integrative way.

Fire Element - The Fire Element is Divinely Masculine and its direction is outward. It represents expansion, authenticity, confidence, belonging, empowerment, community and connection. Fire is connected to the Emotion of Joy, symbolizing your ability to be content with what is.

Five Element Theory - Five Element Theory is an ancient philosophical tradition from East Asia (Japan, Korea and China). It categorizes the archetypal energies in the Universe as Elements, namely: Water, Wood, Fire, Earth and Metal. It is connected to the way of life called Taoism.

Harmony - to live in alignment with your natural cycles.

Higher Self - The aspect of you that only speaks the language of love. It is whole and a direct slice of Universal Consciousness. It does not know linear time, but infinite time. Your Highest Self always has free will and is always in communication with you. You are never disconnected from this part of self. Yet, sometimes we can be distracted or forget. Your Highest Self ensures you stay on your life path to learn your soul's curriculum in this lifetime.

Indigenous - to be native to one's land, living in harmony with and tending to the Earth for a sustainable future, keeping the well-being of all species for generations to come in mind when making choices

Inner Autumn - the divine feminine season of life when you are navigating the themes of releasing attachment, sustaining meaningful relationships, exploring attachment styles, forgiveness, grief, presence, preciousness, self worth, healing from the Father Wound, emotionally releasing/letting go, or navigating dying or death in any capacity. The emotional teacher during this Season is Grief. The energy of this season flows in a downward direction. It is associated with the Lung and Large Intestine meridians. The meditative color is white.

Inner Spring - the divine masculine season of life when you are navigating the themes of intention setting, organization, trial and error, obstacles, gaining momentum, healthy and balanced structure and planning. The emotional teacher during this Season is Anger. The energy of this season flows in an upward direction. It is associated with the Liver and Gallbladder meridians. The meditative color is green.

Inner Summer - the divine masculine season of life when you are navigating the themes of being seen, expressing your authentic self, expansion, community, belonging, play, pleasure, inner teen healing, desire, sensuality, sexuality and confidence. The emotional teacher during this time is Joy. The energy of this season flows outward. It is associated with the Heart, San Jiao, Heart Protector and Small Intestine Meridians. The meditative color is yellow.

Inner Winter - the divine feminine season of life

when you are navigating the themes of introspection, rest, daydreaming, trauma healing, limiting beliefs, subconscious rewiring, fear, anxiety, trust, surrender, intuition, wisdom and courage. The emotional teacher during this Season is Fear. The energy of this season flows inward. It is associated with the Kidney and Urinary Bladder meridians. The meditative color is deep blue, deep purple or black.

Integration - to make whole; to remember one's wholeness.

Magic - the power of influencing the course of events by using mysterious or supernatural forces. This spelling is typically reserved for fictional fantasy novels and films.

Magick - the process of aligning oneself with natural forces to manifest an intention; the power of transforming your life through applying Inner Alchemy practices. Paganism originally spelled this word this way, referring to ritual techniques that change a person's consciousness so that he or she may better perceive and participate in divine reality.

Metal Element - The Metal Element is a Divinely Feminine Element and its direction is downwards. It represents the themes of letting in, letting go, emotional liberation, preciousness, self worth and the maturity of your inner father archetype. Its ruling Emotion is Grief, symbolizing your ability to let love in and practice nonattachment in a harmonious way.

Parts Work - the process of having an internal dialogue (such as through thought or journaling) with the different 'parts' of self. Some parts may disagree and this is a big source of suffering. Through having such a dialogue, with your Highest Self mediating, one can find internal resolution, peace and safety.

Regulation - when the nervous system, fascial system

and body feel safe. Regulation cannot be controlled by the cognitive mind, rather it is a felt-sense experience.

Repatterning - the Inner Alchemy process of transforming belief systems to be in harmonious alignment with one's authentic Self (the Higher Self). This is done through embodiment/somatic practices as our beliefs live in the body.

Shadow - any thought patterns, beliefs, or habits you've unconsciously adopted as a strategy to receive basic needs like love, attention, care or support. You can consider your shadow to be a part of you. When one is integrated with their shadow, they are liberated and more authentic, as the goal is not to remove the Shadow but befriend it. When one is unconscious of what resides in their shadow, the shadow usually filters their life to mirror back what is within it creating patterns. Your shadow is usually developed early in life, specifically during childhood and is typically unconscious unless one does Shadow Work or Inner Alchemy processes.

Shadow Trigger - when a stimulus triggers you to an emotional state that is energetically not matched to the situation at hand.

Space Between (The) - the divine feminine season of life when you are navigating the themes of your relationship to your physical body, money, food, abundance, stability, compassion, giving and receiving, and healing the Mother wound. The emotional teacher during this Season is Empathy. The energy of this season is neutral and flows neither up, down, out or in. It is associated with the Stomach and Spleen meridians. The meditative color is yellow.

Spirit Guides - your Spirit Guides are high vibrational entities that hold wisdom, guidance and unconditional love for you. Because we are all One

Consciousness, they are a part of you. When navigating times of self doubt, you can refer to your Guides for assistance. They love when you ask for help!

Spiritual - believing in something more multi-faceted and grander than the individual ego self

Soul - The part of you that never dies. It has a slight "personality" from the many lifetimes you have lived. This part of you carries your karma which are patterns that you carry between lifetimes. The soul incarnates in order to learn a particular curriculum, similar to studying a "major" or "minor" in college. Your soul can incarnate on places like Earth or other planets, star systems or dimensions. It is said that your soul can be in multiple places at once, meaning incarnate in lifetimes that are happening parallel to this one. The primary mission of your soul is to learn, grow, evolve and transmit information to Source Consciousness.

Starseed - a soul that has incarnated in lifetimes that are other than Earth. Examples may include Orion, Pleiadean, Lyran, Venusian, Martian, Andromedan, Arcturian, Mintakan

Subconscious - the fascial and nervous system; emotional "tape recorder" of all life events/feelings; storehouse of one's values, beliefs, morals, creative impulses, desires and emotional patterns; some believe the word 'Soul' to be interchangeable with 'Subconscious'

The Universe - interchangeable for God, Goddess, Universal Consciousness, Source Consciousness, Great Spirit, Krishna, Allah, Elohim, Christ Consciousness, etc. It is a part of you and every single thing you see on this planet. It is simultaneously "no-thing."

Water Element - The Water Element is a Divinely Feminine Element and its direction is inwards. It represents your intuition, trust, surrender, inner safety, and the nervous system. The ruling Emotion is Fear and symbolizes your ability to alchemize trauma for wisdom.

Wood Element - The Wood Element is a Divinely Masculine Element and its direction is upwards. It represents your thinking mind, organizing your thoughts, planning ahead, finding direction and inspiring motivation. The ruling Emotion is Anger and symbolizes your ability to alchemize stagnation into aligned action.

Yang - see divine masculine

Yin - see divine feminine

THANK YOU

Sweet soul, thank you for trusting me to guide you through the path of *The Akashic Alchemist*. It is such a blessing to be awakening together in this lifetime. If you'd like to explore more depth and soulful expansion, I invite you to explore my 1:1 mentorship programs, online courses, retreats, workshops and ceremonies. To learn more about my offerings and explore ways we can work together, please visit www.carleenalarayoga.com.

Gifting this book to a friend or writing a review on Goodreads.com, Amazon amzn.to/3Np7871 or wherever you purchased your book is one of the most appreciated gifts you can send back to an author.

If you'd like to stay in touch, be sure to follow on social media @carleena.la.curandera and @the.akashic.alchemist. If you prefer to do it old school, you can email me carleena@theakashicalchemist.com. I love hearing from readers and building community, so don't be shy to drop in and say hello! It would be my pleasure to connect with you. And remember: *you are the alchemist.* I cannot wait to see what magick you create!

Lots of Love,

Carleena

Beana

JOURNEY DEEPER

This book has been formatted into a living body of work that you can access online using the QR code or website below. There you will find free embodiment practices, guided meditations, downloadable PDFs and more to support your alchemical journey. You can also explore Carlena's podcast, YouTube channel, Insight Timer app meditation profile, Instagram and more. If you wish to share feedback or ask questions, you can find Carleena's contact information in the links below. She loves to hear from readers so feel free to reach out! If you loved this book, consider taking a moment to leave a review on Goodreads and Amazon, or wherever you purchased your book. Leaving reviews is one of the best ways to support authors and promotes visibility of their work.

If you'd like to cultivate a sustainable and transformational alchemical path, consider enrolling in The Akashic Alchemist Wisdom Portal: an online school dedicated to empowerment, liberation and Inner Alchemy. We have courses with varying topics and intentions to support you and new content is added routinely.

The Book's Website:

www.carleenalarayoga.com/the-akashic-alchemist

Website Password: *Alchemist999*

Linktree: *linktr.ee/theakashicalchemist*

(see QR code to scan)

ACKNOWLEDGMENTS

I'd like to first thank the incredible team at Red Thread Publishing. I manifested the discovery of a women-owned publishing company that teaches a cyclical living writing process to publish this book about cyclical living. How synchronistic! Thank you to my developmental editor Mimi who gave me such grounded feedback and for working with me when my draft was in her infancy. I see your heart of service to this work and the publishing of women's voices. Deep gratitude to my copy editor Adrienne who applied her creative genius to the polished version you are reading today. And I must thank Sarah, from the bottom of my heart, for introducing me to the Red Thread Community.

Thank you to my lucky number 7: Alyssa, Maggie, Sierra, Keight, Yvonne, Bernadette and Seana. You were the first people to step into the process of *The Akashic Alchemist*. Your trust, faith and devotion to the process allowed this book to come alive for the first time and for that I'll always remember our special time together.

A special thank you to Jonny who allowed our lives to

unfold in accordance to our authentic heart's desires and continuing to love me, regardless. I couldn't have finished this book without your unwavering support during those difficult days of uncertainty and doubt.

To my beautiful family who continued to show up with encouragement and affirmation, thank you for loving me during the tender process of writing my first book and making me laugh along the way. A special thank you to my mom, who was never short of good ideas. Thank you for believing in me that I'd write a book some day and for encouraging me to step into doing my soul's work full time. To my dad (Papi) who taught me the importance of talking to the moon, plants and the Earth. To my brother, thank you for stretching the edges of my intelligence with our debates and philosophical discussions. I thought of things from all angles because of your inspiration. And to my baby sister who is the only one who knew the depth of our childhood. Thank you for being the best partner to explore the land around our family's rancher with. The imaginary realms we created together brought me much needed joy in those early years of life. I hope that this book supports Ayla and our lineage someday.

Thank you to the ancestors who stepped forward as I wrote this book, offering me wisdom, lessons, and sometimes hard truths. I am proud of our ancestral lineage that is rich with culture, history and vibrancy. May this book be a homage to all of your sacrifices and dedication to your children and their children's children.

Thank you to the Mexica people of México who have welcomed me with open arms into your culture, traditions and ceremonial gatherings. I hope that this book showcases the inspiration, guidance and dedication to the land, your elders and your traditions that you have instilled within me. I see this world as a precious living being more so because of your perspective to see the present as precious. I am proud to call myself *una Danzante de Luna*. A special thank you to my lil' moon dumplings who showed me what unconditional love is in sisterhood circle. It's an honor to pray with you in sacred service to humanity every full moon. *Ollinmalinalmetztli!*

Gratitude to the Nanticoke Lenni-Lenape peoples of southern New Jersey for stewarding the land long before I was born, preserving this Garden State of New Jersey. Thank you to all Indigenous groups who have tended to the land long before my ancestors arrived. It is my greatest hope that reparations and restitution of land will be offered to the original caretakers within my lifetime, as an offering of justice and hope for our future. To Mother Earth and all the lands I wrote this book upon: thank you for teaching me through the magnificent lessons you channeled through me. Thank you to all the Elemental Spirits of the Earth, of Fire, Air, Earth, Water and Ether. I am forever your student.

Thank you to Paramahansa Yogananda, Abuela Malinali, Mother Mary, Yeshua, Mary Magdalene, Isis, Kuan Yin, Green Tara, White Buffalo Calf Woman, Hathor and my entire Council of Light. I hope that this book carries your message of unconditional love in devotion to the rising of consciousness on this planet and beyond.

SOURCES

1. A., V. der K. B. (2015). The body keeps the score: Mind, brain and body in the transformation of trauma. Penguin Books.
2. Araminta. (2020, July 13). Polyvagal theory: Coregulation. Khiron Clinics. khironclinics.com/blog/polyvagal-theory-coregulation .
3. Bertrand, A. (2017). Womb awakening: Initiatory Wisdom from the Creatrix of all life. Bear & Company.
4. Dana, D., & Porges, S. W. (2018). In The polyvagal theory in therapy: Engaging the rhythm of regulation. essay, W.W. Norton & Company.
5. Environmental Protection Agency. (2021, September 7). Indoor Air Quality. What are the trends in indoor air quality and their effects on human health? www.epa.gov/report-environment/indoor-air-quality
6. Franklin, P. by B. (2022, October 17). This fall,

leave the leaves! www.usda.gov/media/blog/2022/10/17/fall-leave-leaves

7. Gale, M. S. (2021, July 20). Water: An indigenous perspective meets contemporary science. Tribal Trust Foundation. tribaltrustfoundation.org/life/water-an-indigenous-perspective-meets-contemporary-science

8. Hall, D. (2018, April 18). The Navajo Concept of Wind. repository.gatech.edu/server/api/core/bitstreams/236fcfad-2428-477c-90ff-d9fefc4a0f19/content

9. Ho, W. W. (2022). Influence of play on positive psychological development in emerging adulthood: A serial mediation model. Frontiers in Psychology, 13. doi.org/10.3389/fpsyg.2022.1057557

10. Hwang, T.-J., Rabheru, K., Peisah, C., Reichman, W., & Ikeda, M. (2020). Loneliness and social isolation during the COVID-19 pandemic. International Psychogeriatrics, 32(10), 1217–1220. doi.org/10.1017/s1041610220000988

11. Inter-Tribal Council of Michigan. (n.d.). Zisbakwtoke Gises Maple Sugar Moon. itcmi.org/wp-content/uploads/2023/02/2P-Zisbakwtoke-Gises-Maple-Sugar-Moon.pdf

12. Jarrett, L. S. (2009). Nourishing destiny: The Inner Tradition of Chinese Medicine. Spirit Path Press.

13. Kaparo, R. (2012). Awakening somatic

intelligence: The art and practice of embodied mindfulness. North Atlantic.

14. Kimmerer, R. W. (2022). Chapter 16: Maple Nation: A Citizenship Guide. In Braiding Sweetgrass (pp. 167–174). chapter, Langara College.

15. Krulwich, R. (2012, June 22). How do plants know which way is up and which way is down?. NPR. www.npr.org/sections/krulwich/2012/06/21/ 155508849/how-do-plants-know-which-way-is-up-and-which-way-is-down

16. Le Pertel, N., Fisher, J., & van Dam, N. (2020). Neuroscience of Embodied Reflection: Somatic/Mindbody/contemplative practices, health, and transformative learning. Reflective Practice, 21(6), 803–818. doi.org/10.1080/14623943.2020.1827492

17. National Geographic. (2021, May 4). Thirsty Food. Freshwater 101: Food. www.nationalgeographic.com/environment/article/thirsty-food

18. Oschman, J. L., Chevalier, G., & Brown, R. (2015, March 24). The effects of grounding (earthing) on inflammation, the immune response, wound healing, and prevention and treatment of chronic inflammatory and autoimmune diseases. Journal of inflammation research. www.ncbi.nlm.nih.gov/pmc/articles/PMC4378297/

19. Pollack Laboratory. (n.d.). Research. pollacklab. www.pollacklab.org/research

20. Radin, D., Hayssen, G., Emoto, M., & Kizu, T. (2006). Double-blind test of the effects of distant intention on Water Crystal Formation.

EXPLORE, 2(5), 408–411.
doi.org/10.1016/j.explore.2006.06.004

21. Richard Grant. (2018, March 1). Do trees talk to each other? A controversial German forester says yes, and his ideas are shaking up the scientific world. Science. www.smithsonianmag.com/science-nature/the-whispering-trees-180968084/

22. T;, R. D. G. M. (2006). Double-blind test of the effects of distant intention on Water Crystal Formation. Explore (New York, N.Y.). pubmed.ncbi.nlm.nih.gov/16979104/

23. Tutu, D., Gyatso, T., & Abrams, D. (2016). Book of joy: Lasting happiness in a Changing World. Cornerstone Publishers.

24. UN Environmental Program. (2022, November 24). The environmental costs of Fast Fashion. UNEP. www.unep.org/news-and-stories/story/environmental-costs-fast-fashion

25. UNICEF-IRC. (2019, June). Are the world's richest countries family friendly? Are the world's richest countries family friendly?: Policy in the OECD and EU. www.unicef-irc.org/family-friendly

26. United Nations. (n.d.). Background: Technical platform on the measurement and reduction of food loss and waste: Food and Agriculture Organization of the United Nations. Food and Agriculture Organization. www.fao.org/platform-food-loss-waste/background/en

27. University of Cambridge. (n.d.). The origins of the universe: Inflation. Centre for Theoretical Cosmology: The Origins of the Universe:

Inflation Introduction. www.ctc.cam.ac.uk/outreach/origins/inflation _zero.php

28. Why compost?. Garden State Composting. (n.d.). www.gardenstatecomposting.com/why-compost

29. World Health Organization. (n.d.). Maternity protection: Compliance with International Labour Standards. Maternity protection: Compliance with international labour standards. www.who.int/data/nutrition/nlis/info/maternity-protection-compliance-with-international-labour-standards

ENDNOTES

INTRODUCTION

1. Le Pertel, N., Fisher, J. & van Dam, N. (2020a). Neuroscience of Embodied Reflection: Somatic/Mindbody/contemplative practices, health, and transformative learning. Reflective Practice, 21(6), 803–818.

THE MAGICK OF WATER

1. Radin, D., Hayssen, G., Emoto, M., & Kizu, T. (2006). Double-blind test of the effects of distant intention on Water Crystal Formation. EXPLORE, 2(5), 408–411.
2. Gale, M. S. (2021, July 20). Water: An indigenous perspective meets contemporary science. Tribal Trust Foundation.
3. Radin, D., Hayssen, G., Emoto, M., & Kizu, T. (2006). Double-blind test of the effects of distant intention on Water Crystal Formation. EXPLORE, 2(5), 408–411.

WHAT IF FEAR BECAME YOUR TEACHER?

1. Dana, D., & Porges, S. W. (2018). In The polyvagal theory in therapy: Engaging the rhythm of regulation. essay, W.W. Norton & Company.

THE MAGICK OF WOOD

1. Kimmerer, R. W. (2022). Chapter 16: Maple Nation: A Citizenship Guide. In Braiding Sweetgrass (pp. 167–174). chapter, Langara College.
2. Inter-Tribal Council of Michigan. (n.d.). Zisbakwtoke Gises Maple Sugar Moon.
3. Krulwich, R. (2012, June 22). How do plants know which way is up and which way is down?. NPR.
4. Hall, D. (2018, April 18). The Navajo Concept of Wind.

5. Richard Grant. (2018, March 1). Do trees talk to each other? A controversial German forester says yes, and his ideas are shaking up the scientific world. Science.

ALCHEMY OF INNER SPRING

1. Sahakian, B.J., & Labuzetta, J. (2013). Bad Moves: How decision making goes wrong, and the ethics of smart drugs.

WHAT IS INNER SUMMER?

1. Tutu, D., Gyatso, T., & Abrams, D. (2016). Book of joy: Lasting happiness in a Changing World. Cornerstone Publishers.

THE MAGICK OF FIRE

1. For reference, that's multiplying the size of a peach by 10,000,000,000,000,000,000,000,000,000,000,000,000,000,000,000,000,000,000,000,000,00,000,000,000,000,000 in less than *one second*.
2. University of Cambridge. (n.d.). The origins of the universe: Inflation. Centre for Theoretical Cosmology: The Origins of the Universe: Inflation Introduction.

ALCHEMY OF INNER SUMMER

1. Hwang, T.-J., Rabheru, K., Peisah, C., Reichman, W., & Ikeda, M. (2020). Loneliness and social isolation during the COVID-19 pandemic. International Psychogeriatrics, 32(10), 1217–1220.
2. Araminta. (2020, July 13). Polyvagal theory: Coregulation. Khiron Clinics.
3. Ho, W. W. (2022). Influence of play on positive psychological development in emerging adulthood: A serial mediation model. Frontiers in Psychology, 13.

THE MAGICK OF EARTH

1. UNICEF-IRC. (2019, June). Are the world's richest countries family friendly? Are the world's richest countries family friendly?: Policy in the OECD and EU.

WHAT IS INNER AUTUMN?

1. Jarrett, L. S. (2009). Nourishing destiny: The inner tradition of Chinese medicine. Spirit Path Press.

THE MAGICK OF METAL

1. All clients' names have been changed for confidentiality.

RE-INDIGENIZE YOUR RELATIONSHIP WITH THE EARTH

1. Environmental Protection Agency. (2021, September 7). Indoor Air Quality. What are the trends in indoor air quality and their effects on human health?
2. Oschman, J. L., Chevalier, G., & Brown, R. (2015, March 24). The effects of grounding (earthing) on inflammation, the immune response, wound healing, and prevention and treatment of chronic inflammatory and autoimmune diseases. Journal of inflammation research.
3. United Nations. (n.d.). Background: Technical platform on the measurement and reduction of food loss and waste: Food and Agriculture Organization of the United Nations. Food and Agriculture Organization.
4. Why compost?. Garden State Composting. (n.d.).
5. Franklin, P. by B. (2022, October 17). This fall, leave the leaves!
6. UN Environmental Program. (2022, November 24). The environmental costs of Fast Fashion. UNEP.
7. National Geographic. (2021, May 4). Thirsty Food. Freshwater 101: Food.
8. Bertrand, A. (2017). Womb awakening: Initiatory Wisdom from the Creatrix of all life. Bear & Company.

A CALL TO ACTION

1. United Nations. (n.d.). About indigenous peoples and human rights. The Office of the High Commissioner for Human Rights. www.ohchr.org/en/indigenous-peoples/about-indigenous-peoples-and-human-rights

2. U.S. Department of Interior. (n.d.). Missing and Murdered Indigenous People Crisis. Indian Affairs. www.bia.gov/service/mmu/missing-and-murdered-indigenous-people-crisis

3. U.S. Department of Interior. (n.d.). Missing and Murdered Indigenous People Crisis. Indian Affairs. www.bia.gov/service/mmu/missing-and-murdered-indigenous-people-crisis

4. Survival International. (n.d.). Indigenous people are the best conservationists. Decolonize conservation. www.survivalinternational.org/conservation

ABOUT THE AUTHOR

▽ .

Carleena Lara Bregatta is an author, spiritual coach, and embodiment mentor. She teaches people how to return to the ancient art of cyclical living, sharing tools on how to inner resource safety, sovereignty and freedom. Her creative work weaves together modern neuroscience with Five Element Theory and Tantrik Yogic Philosophy for a multi-faceted approach to trauma healing, self-empowerment and soulful self-discovery. She is the host of *The Akashic Alchemist: A Spiritual Podcast* where she teaches through the ancient ways of storytelling and alchemy.

Carleena is a certified Usui Reiki Master, 800 Hour E-RYT (Experienced Registered Yoga Teacher), a certified hypnotherapist & past life regression therapist, a somatic embodiment coach and holds a B.A. in Psychology and an M.A. in International Relations. She has been teaching yoga and meditation for ten years and routinely facilitates yoga teacher trainings, reiki attunements, group immersions and retreats across the United States and internationally.

"Magick is not something you do. Magick is something you are."
- Donald Michael Kraig

Made in the USA
Middletown, DE
23 June 2023

33256276R00179